why men

never remember

and

women

never forget

why men

never remember

and

women

never forget

MARIANNE J. LEGATO,
MD, FACP

**FOUNDER OF THE PARTNERSHIP FOR GENDER-SPECIFIC MEDICINE
AT COLUMBIA UNIVERSITY
AND AUTHOR OF *EVE'S RIB* AND *THE FEMALE HEART***

WITH LAURA TUCKER

RODALE

© 2005 by Marianne J. Legato

Printed in the United States of America

Rodale Inc. makes every effort to use acid-free ∞, recycled paper ♻.

Book design by Joanna Williams

Library of Congress Cataloging-in-Publication Data

Legato, Marianne J., date.
 Why men never remember and women never forget / Marianne J. Legato with Laura Tucker.
  p.   cm.
 Includes index.
 ISBN-13 978–1–57954–897–1 hardcover
 ISBN-10 1–57954–897–0 hardcover
 1. Sex differences (Psychology)   2. Man-woman relationships.   I. Tucker, Laura, date.
II. Title.
BF692.2.L45   2005
155.3'3—dc22   2005014784

Distributed to the trade by Holtzbrinck Publishers

2   4   6   8   10   9   7   5   3   1   hardcover

To John Pepper, who made it all possible, and from whom I learned much

Contents

Acknowledgments

Warmest thanks to the following individuals:

Richard Curtis, my beloved agent, who convinced me that this book should be written;

Leslie Curtis, whose finely honed intelligence set a clear course for me when I found the road difficult to navigate;

Heather Jackson and Tami Booth, my editors at Rodale, whose enthusiasm for the project never flagged;

Laura Tucker, who helped make my scientific prose accessible to all of you;

Christiana Killian, whose ability to communicate has taught me the value of clarity, content, and charm in making any point.

Introduction:

The Anatomy of a Quarrel

Liz walks in the house to find her husband watching football in the den, while their toddler plays at his feet. She can tell that Ella has logged some serious playground hours from the sweaty smell that greets her as she leans over for a kiss. "Did you have a big day at the park, sweetheart? Did you have fun on the slide?"

The house is a disaster, and they're expected at Tim's parents' house with as-yet unbaked cookies in an hour. Liz dials a colleague's number as she takes ingredients out of the fridge. Phone cradled to her ear, she learns that an e-mail with important information for tomorrow's meeting still hasn't arrived. She relays a modification to their upcoming presentation as she adds chocolate chips to the batter.

Cookies in the oven, Liz heads toward the bedroom, stripping as she goes. She calls to Tim over her shoulder, "Will you get Ella ready to go? I've left her dress and shoes out."

When Liz emerges, she finds Tim pacing impatiently by the door. Leaning over to adjust Ella's dress, she sees a sticky patch in her daughter's hair. "You cleaned her up, right?" she asks. "Yes," Tim says, exasperated. "We're late. Let's go."

But when Liz reaches over to take Ella out of her car seat at her in-laws' house, she catches a whiff of that same coppery, sweaty "playground" smell. On inspection, Ella's pudgy hands, filled with Cheerios, are gray with grime.

"Her hands are filthy, Tim!" Liz hisses.

"I'll deal with it when we get inside," he says, bewildered by her tone. Liz feels her growing irritation spill over into rage. "That's not the point, Tim. Why didn't you see how dirty she was when you were changing her? Look at her face! She needed a bath. This means that she's been eating dirt the whole time, which is completely disgusting, not to mention unsafe. What's wrong with you?"

Tim turns on his heel, jaw set, and stalks into the house. Kids eat dirt; she'll survive. Liz follows him, but her torrent of reproaches prompts no reply from her stony-faced husband.

Once they've settled into the party, Tim recovers his equilibrium, but finds that his wife won't respond to his attempts at conversation. More confounded than empathetic, he engages his uncle in a heated and detailed discussion of the day's presidential press conference; within moments, the political discussion has completely eclipsed Liz's distress in his mind.

Tim's sister, on the other hand, takes one look at Liz's flushed face and dilated pupils and pulls her into the kitchen for a hug and a chat. "I can't believe him!" Liz fumes. "She looked like something out of *Oliver Twist*! What was he thinking, putting her in a party dress without even bothering to take a swipe at her face and hands with a washcloth?!"

The case against Tim builds. "Lead levels in the soil in our neighborhood are astronomical. As if we didn't get enough of a scare after the renovation, when the first tests came back high for lead. Does he want her to have brain damage?"

And builds. "I asked him to put her in her dress. I asked if he'd cleaned her up. How much more specific do I have to be? When I leave her with him, do I have to remind him *not* to put her in the oven too?"

Liz is on a slow simmer for the rest of the night. She goes over and over the argument in her head on the drive home. Unable to sleep, she reviews the notes for the following day's presentation, still analyzing the argument in the back of her mind.

The next morning, Liz rebuffs Tim's invitation to make love and arrives at the breakfast table determined to find some kind of resolution. As usual, Tim resists any attempt to have a substantive discussion about the argument or what it means for their relationship. "He doesn't care about me," Liz thinks miserably. "He doesn't care that I'm unhappy."

In fact, Tim doesn't even really know why she's mad. "Why," he wonders for the hundredth time, "does every little thing have to turn into a full-blown drama? Why does she have to make such a big deal out of everything? And why, when it's over, can't she just move on?"

The Sex-Specific Brain: What It Means for Human Relationships

Seen one way, Liz's fight with Tim is nothing more than a commonplace, garden-variety marital spat. But in another light, it perfectly typifies what so often goes wrong between men and women, and why.

We're Different!

Liz and Tim don't have a bad marriage, but when they fight like this, they feel completely alienated from one another. "I can't understand how we can see the same things so differently. It's like he's another species entirely," she says. Tim's not an alien; they're just *different.* Our mistake, whether we're male or female, is to want—to insist, hanker for, demand—us to be alike. And the simple, irrefutable, fabulous fact is that *we are not.*

The differences between males and females are dramatic and in-controvertible to anyone who's even casually observed animals. My male pug is bigger, stronger, and much more active than his sister. While she spends hours quietly wrapped around my feet and hides if she knows it's cold or raining outside, he wanders through the house in search of a favorite toy, nips at her leg to encourage her to get up and play with him, and loves to go out for walks, taking on every pigeon in his path.

Why are they different? Over the past decade, there has been a crescendo of interest in exploring the precise nature and importance of the differences between men and women. The new science of gender-specific medicine is producing an amazing appreciation of how our biological sex modifies the way we operate in the world—and even our experience of disease. We are different, and vastly so, in *every system of the body,* from the skin that covers us, to the hearts that beat within our chests, to the guts that process the food we eat.

Nowhere is this more true than in the brain, the 3-pound organ that houses all that makes us human: our passions, our insights, our appreciation of the created world, our entire intellectual and emotional lives.

Men and women think differently, approach problems differently, emphasize the importance of things differently, and experience the world around us through entirely different filters.

Starting in the womb, and for as long as our lives last, we receive information into sex-specific brains that are significantly different in anatomy, chemical composition, blood flow, and metabolism. The very systems we use to produce ideas and emotions, to create memories, to conceptualize and internalize our experiences, and to solve problems are different.

How come we didn't know this before? Because scientists didn't study women; they studied only men. It has been only at the insistence of women themselves that researchers have been permitted (and indeed encouraged) to look at them directly. The result of this tremendous new step in investigative medicine is that we now have the science to confirm what we knew all along: Men and women are not the same.

I believe that the differences between us offer a key clue to the disconnect that sometimes happens between men and women. I'd like to show you what I mean, so let's go back and look—not at who's right and who's wrong—but at the "anatomy" of the argument that began this chapter.

What's *really* happening when Liz and Tim fight?

Anatomy of an Argument: The Postmortem

Within seconds of her arrival home, Liz's body is in full battle readiness. As she processes each new stressor—the untidy house, the unmade cookies, the errant e-mail—her brain signals for hormones to help her cope with the stress, by raising her blood pressure and pushing her heart to beat at a rate almost twice what's normal. In women, the amygdala, the part of the brain that receives and responds to stressors, has extensive connections to the parts of the brain that control blood pressure and heart rate. Men, on the other hand, have a less extensive network; Tim is engrossed in his game, untouched by stress.

Left to his own devices, and given the time crunch, Tim would probably say to forget the cookies because there will surely be enough food at the party without their contribution. But Liz releases a very im-

portant hormone called oxytocin that motivates her to make and preserve connections with other people, especially those who can help her
with Ella, like Tim's parents. Levels of this hormone are especially high
when women are under stress—making oxytocin a gender-specific and
powerful tool that helps women to meet challenges by recruiting
others. In this case, the hormone powers Liz to go the extra mile by
making a batch of cookies to facilitate bonding.

Liz has more gray matter in the frontal cortex of her brain, the area
just behind the eyes, than Tim does. This is the executive center of the
brain, the CEO that controls our complex behaviors. Liz also has more
connections between the two sides of her brain, which may explain how
she processes several different streams of information at the same
time—modifying her presentation while following a recipe, for instance, or endlessly analyzing her argument with Tim while going over
her notes. Tim, for the most part, activates only one side of his brain
when processing information. This means that he deals with one thing
at a time: He identifies a problem, comes up with a solution, and
moves on. That's one of the reasons he hasn't paid better attention to
Ella's needs: His answer to the "problem"—that they're going to be
late to the party—is to get the child dressed as quickly as possible.

Liz, of course, focuses on a different problem: Ella's dirty hands. Her
larger executive center accesses this as a threat. It sends a message to
the part of the brain that helps us to create memories from our experiences and to the part that stores our memories of emotionally charged
experiences—like the results of Ella's earlier lead test, which came back
high after their apartment renovation.

Tim was afraid for Ella then too, but the experience was *quantita-
tively more unpleasant* for Liz than it was for him because of her biology.
Women have higher levels of the hormone estrogen than men do, and
estrogen does two things when women are under stress. First, it pro-

longs the secretion of the stress hormone, cortisol, so a woman feels more stressed in the moment than a man in the same situation. Estrogen also activates a larger field of neurons in the brain than is the case with men; these activated cells provide women with the network needed to form a much more detailed memory of the sequence of events. So Liz's hormone levels guarantee that she actually has *a more detailed and more vivid memory of the event than Tim does.* This evolutionary adaptation allows her to take good care of Ella by remembering dangerous situations so she can avoid them in the future.

We can see the differences between Liz and Tim in the way they fight too. Liz's left brain, the seat of our ability to process language, has more gray matter than Tim's does, and she uses both sides of her brain for speech, while Tim uses only one. These factors may explain Liz's rich, fluid accusations and Tim's corresponding retreat into silence. We see those verbal skills at work as well in Liz's rhetorical questions to Ella about her day at the park. It's Liz's biological "job" to push the pre-verbal Ella toward language.

That superior ability to communicate also explains how Tim's sister is able to pick up on Liz's distress right away. Women have to be better at reading the subtle and nuanced language of human expression than men, so that they can better determine the needs of their highly dependent, wordless infants. And as we'll see, the bonding that takes place between the two women is a good example of a female behavior pattern in the face of stress; it serves as a better form of self-protection than the typical male "fight or flight" response.

I could go on and on, but you can see how complicated even this routine domestic conflict really is, and how sex-specific.

But what does it all mean?

If men and women are fundamentally, biologically different, what do those differences mean for the ultimate fate of our relationships? Are

Liz and Tim destined to retreat to their sex-specific behaviors and biologically-informed brains, to glare angrily at each other over their grubby child?

Hopefully not. I sincerely believe that a better understanding of the differences between us and a genuine attempt to learn from our partners' best coping strategies will help us narrow the gap.

The Shape of Things to Come

It's clear that many of our behaviors have their roots in our biology, a biology that we now understand to be sex-specific. But some very new science—so stunning that it won its discoverer a Nobel Prize—shows that for all creatures with a nervous system, the experiences we have of the world around us change the very structure of our brains. In other words, your brain will be changed by the very act of reading this book!

If experience changes brain chemistry and structure, and if the brain is the source of all human behavior, then men and women can learn a great deal from each other, changing their own brains in profound ways. Simply understanding the differences between us allows us to *celebrate those differences,* instead of bumping up against them. Each sex has something valuable to offer. Indeed, many of the same differences that cause us conflict in relationships also cause us joy; isn't the contrast between his rough cheek and your smooth one at least part of what makes kissing so delicious?

But this new research makes me wonder if we can't push this process one step further. If practicing piano or gymnastics changes our brains so that we get better at those skills, might we not be able to change our brains as well by "practicing" the competencies of the other sex? We no longer have to wonder at the vast chasm that separates us: Let us instead take advantage of the brain's natural plasticity and use it to become more alike.

I take as my inspiration a fish called the blue-headed wrasse. If a female blue-headed wrasse is the largest in her group, and there are no male wrasses around, she will change her behavior to that of a male fish within minutes of the discovery. Her female reproductive organs change more slowly but will become male within days after the behavioral change. We humans have a hormone called vasopressin, an analog of the brain chemical in the fish that instigates the behavioral change. Might we too be able to switch between the sexes—or at least between their dominant characteristics—if the environment demanded it?

I am not the only one to be inspired by the blue-headed wrasse; she is the muse behind Elaine May's play *The Way of All Fish*, about a power reversal between two women, a high-powered executive and her secretary. Imagine choosing our sex according to what might work best in a given situation or just on the basis of our moods. I'd definitely choose to be male when negotiating for more support or money from the deans at Columbia, and I'd choose to be female the minute I left work to come home to my family.

Ultimately, I believe that this metamorphosis is already happening, as the opportunities for women become more like the ones that are available for men and as our experiences become more similar. I do believe—and research by Eric Kandel, MD, a professor at Columbia University College of Physicians and Surgeons in New York City, supports my hypothesis—that the changing roles of women and men in our society make us more alike, blurring the distinction between prototypically male and female behavior. Indeed, many of us are discovering that the old rules don't apply, as we negotiate a post–World War II world that finds many dads manning the preschool bake sale, while mommies rush off to the investment bank.

As we learn from one another, and in that way become more like each other, I believe we make it possible to live up to our potential in the world and to communicate more effectively with our partners in love and work—instead of firing at each other across the trenches.

This belief is behind the way I have written this book. Much of what I have written is an overview of the research dealing with the differences between us—whether those differences are the result of our unique biology or of the society and culture that shapes us—and how those differences impact our relationships in their various phases at different times in our lives. It is interesting to see how our perspective on these differences change: The same contrasts that may make someone seem very attractive to us in a courtship phase may give rise to disagreements further down the road when we're parenting together. (A note: I have followed the usual progression of these things, although I certainly know that people sometimes have sex before love, or without it altogether, and many couples opt not to have children.) Because I believe that we can change—and because of this fantastic new research that shows we can change on the most fundamental level of all—I have threaded prescriptive advice throughout, designed to help you navigate the conflicts that sometimes come about as a result of these differences.

You may be wondering what qualifies me to write this book; after all, I'm trained as a cardiologist and an internist, not a brain specialist or a relationship expert. I have, however, been involved in the field of gender-specific medicine since its inception. In the eighties and nineties, there was a tremendous surge in interest in the field of "women's health." For the most part, it was a marketing effort on the part of doctors and hospitals to cater to women, who make the majority of medical decisions in the family. The science of gender difference was hardly substantive at that point; often this commitment had no more substance than allocating funds toward a geographically separate women's center, staffed with female doctors and nurses, and decorated in pastels. The emphasis tended to be on the usual "bikini view" of women's health: mammograms and Pap smears. There was little or no attention paid to the unique needs of the whole female patient.

In 1991, I wrote a book called *The Female Heart*, which was the first book to look at the way an organ system differed in men and women. It sparked a tremendous amount of interest, and as I traveled around the world to lecture on the topic, I began to wonder myself whether there were important differences in other organs between the sexes. If there were, then it was worth considering not only the way we did research, but the way we treated patients: We would have to acknowledge that men and women were not identical. I didn't know the answer, but it seemed clear to me that someone—someone with rigorous scientific training and standards—would have to answer this question if this new field of gender-specific medicine were to survive.

So in 1997, I went to the chairman of my department at Columbia University and asked for his support in building a program devoted to studying the difference between how men and women experience disease. I obtained financial support from the private sector, led by Procter & Gamble, and the Partnership for Women's Health was born. Since the 1990s, the field of "women's health" has expanded into a much wider and more inclusive concept: gender-specific medicine, the science of the differences between men and women. (Our program's name has changed to the Partnership for Gender-Specific Medicine—as I had wanted from the outset.)

As the result of a decade of research, we know now that the differences between the sexes are legion and the implications so enormously important that we can no longer justify doing research only in men. As the Institute of Medicine's expert committee said, "Sex does matter. It matters in ways that we did not expect. Undoubtedly, it also matters in ways that we have not begun to imagine." In 1998, I founded the very first journal of gender-specific medicine, indexed by the prestigious National Library of Medicine. And in 2004, I edited the first textbook in gender-specific medicine, with more than 220 contributors from all over the world. The field continues to grow, and I am thrilled and excited to be at the forefront.

I had always been interested in the brain; after all, I've made my career by using my own! But my interest was never more intense than when I began to look into the differences between the sexes. In the process, I came across so many "aha" moments ("So *that's* why that happens!") and had such incredible reactions when I shared what I was learning with my friends, patients, and colleagues that I knew something crucially important was happening to medicine and that this information needed to find its way to a wider audience. You are holding the result in your hands.

What Does It Mean to Be Male or Female?

I have taken a number of risks in writing this book, and I wish to acknowledge them right at the outset. For instance, there is a tremendous risk in categorizing certain behaviors as "male" or "female," as I do throughout this book. There is a cautionary skit in *Free to Be You and Me* in which two babies (played to great effect by Marlo Thomas and Mel Brooks) argue about whether they're boys or girls. Boys can keep secrets, and they're not afraid of mice, so the Mel Brooks baby, who can't and is, must definitely be a girl—right? The debate continues until the nurse comes to change their diapers, which settles the matter once and for all.

That is not the only risk I have taken. In many cases, I have used the results of research done with animals to speculate about human behaviors. We can take many clues about our behavior from our friends in the animal kingdom, especially since we can do experiments on animals that we could not ethically do on humans. But taking animal behavior as "evidence" that similar behaviors exist in humans is irresponsible.

Another, similar risk comes from making a jump from anatomy to function. We can make relatively sophisticated observations about brain structure and function in the living brain, but how to interpret those data is a different matter. Greater blood flow in an area of the brain when you say a rhyme doesn't tell us anything about your ability to say it well, remember it later, or anything else. We don't know whether the structural differences in the brain that we're finding mean anything in terms of talents or abilities. Any such leap—especially in an area like the brain, where we know so very little—is nothing more than speculation on my part. To do more than speculate is to commit "bad" science in the truest sense: to make conclusions based on faulty evidence, conclusions that have the potential to send us scrambling in the wrong directions.

Whatever speculation I have engaged in over the course of the pages that follow is in the service of a larger concept: the idea that, whatever our differences, there is much that men and women can learn from one another. I consider this book to be a first look at a new science that may help us to understand the differences between men and women, and to reconcile some of the difficulties that have sprung up between us as the result of those differences. I would encourage you to think of it in the same way.

Whether the challenges are new or as old as time, the differences between us don't have to cause tension and conflict in our relationships. Ultimately, understanding them will help us to buiid closeness and commonality and to learn from each other. We are far more alike than we are different, and there is evidence to suggest that we can cultivate the aptitudes of the opposite sex, to the very great benefit of us all.

1

Men and Women Are Different

True or False?

"**M**ath class is hard!"

So exclaimed Teen Barbie, a talking version of the doll on the market in the early nineties—to the widespread outrage of consumers. (In response, the guerilla-activist group the Barbie Liberation Organization bought a number of the dolls, swapped the voice boxes with those from G.I. Joe dolls, and replaced them on the shelves. I don't know which one I'd rather have: a muscle-bound, gun-toting G.I. Joe, giggling, "Let's plan our dream wedding!" or Barbie, with her impossible body and blank stare, growling, "Vengeance is mine!")

Mattel pulled the doll and replaced the offensive messages, but every woman in this culture knows that these stereotypes are alive and well, both on and off the toy store shelves. Indeed, much of the pressure not to investigate innate differences between men and women come from the women who most valiantly fight for and defend the rights of women. They're apprehensive that what is learned will be used against us—dumbed down in the media to sound bites that misrepresent the science, or more seriously, held up as evidence of our inferiority in political and academic contexts.

So it's with some trepidation that I address the following questions: Are men and women really different? Do they really process information differently? If so, can we conclude that we have sex-specific areas of excellence in problem solving? These questions are where this book must, of necessity, begin. I feel compelled to wade in, trepidations or no, for one simple reason: We empower ourselves through knowledge.

This is something I have seen proven over and over again as I have worked in this nascent field of gender-specific medicine. When I began in this field, we assumed that women were, physiologically speaking, simply small men. Unfortunately, what we didn't know about the differences between the sexes was hurting women.

Misunderstandings about the differences in the way the female heart worked meant that doctors sent women home, mid–heart attack, when they complained of pain centered in their stomachs. Medications tested in men continued to be prescribed to women, even though the drugs made their symptoms worse. In short, overlooking the differences caused doctors to make mistakes. Many women suffered, and some died.

We may still be making those mistakes; our journey toward a sex-specific medicine has only just begun. We've merely started to scratch the surface of how women are anatomically and biologically different from men, and what that means for how we prevent and cure disease and promote wellness in both sexes. Every day, we make discoveries of paramount importance, discoveries that indicate we must diagnose and treat women differently from their male counterparts.

The most unexplored area is the brain. There is sufficient scientific evidence to suggest that women's and men's brains are different, but the full extent of these differences—and their implications—is still uncharted territory. There are neurological and hormonal differences between us, but what do they mean?

Certainly, this has relevance to those who practice medicine in the field. Perhaps what we discover will change the way we treat neurological disorders like Parkinson's disease, developmental disorders like autism, and cognitive dysfunctions like dementia. It is certainly true that we cannot arrive at a complete understanding of any disease state, developmental disturbance, or neurological imbalance without understanding why it affects both sexes differently; and many of these diseases really do affect the sexes differently.

Take schizophrenia, for instance, a disease that some physicians and public health workers think is the most devastating disease in the world—and one from which an estimated 2 million Americans suffer. Why do female schizophrenics have a later onset, longer periods of remission, and better outcomes than men with the disease? Why do female schizophrenics experience an intensification in their symptoms in the days before their menstrual periods? Why do male schizophrenics have a more difficult time recognizing odors than female schizophrenics do? Perhaps these differences between the sexes can provide us with clues to the cause and treatment of this disease in both. Given how important recognizing these differences has been in other fields, I feel that we have no choice but to forge ahead with the research.

But the brain is so strongly associated with behavior that there are inevitable (and in my opinion, very interesting) sociological implications to this research as well. How do the hormonal and neurological differences between us affect the way we live—and live together? If we knew more about what makes our brains different from our male colleagues, sons, and lovers, wouldn't it be easier to live in harmony with them? My investigations in this chapter, and in this book as a whole, are based on that premise.

A Work in Progress—Forever!

I say over and over in this text that men and women have a great deal to learn from one another, and I believe that this is true. I myself have learned a tremendous amount from men: from my father, who was my first teacher, to the predominantly male class I studied with in medical school (I was one of 13 women in a class of 144), to the professors under whom I studied, most of them men.

But some stunning new research shows that learning happens at a much deeper and more fundamental level than we'd thought, and I believe this has fantastically important implications for the way that men and women can learn from one another. The brain is never really completely "done"; our experiences continue to have a profound effect on the structure of this miraculous organ. New research shows that the brain continues to develop past infancy and puberty—indeed, for as long as we live and continue to provide it with stimulation.

Many scientists have contributed to our understanding of how what we experience as we interact with the world affects our brain, but none with such impact as Dr. Eric Kandel, a professor at Columbia University in New York City, where I also teach. Dr. Kandel has shown—through his research on the lowly sea slug, no less!—that learning depends on creating specific circuits of communication in the brain and that these communication circuits are tailored *by what we experience.*

Learning is the process of acquiring information. Memory is the form in which that information is stored so that you can retrieve it at a later date. Dr. Kandel's Nobel-prize winning work showed that the act of learning and remembering causes physical changes in the brain. We remember things and events by making specific groups of neurons communicate more intensely with one another—by increasing the strength of existing connections and/or by making new ones. Dr.

Kandel showed that our experiences actually *modify the structure and function of our brains* to create memories of those experiences, and we use these memories to modify our behavior accordingly.

The nervous system in Dr. Kandel's snail learned because its experience caused an actual change in the physical connections between the nerve cells. Ours does too. The intensity of the communication between the cells of our brains changes because of actual changes within those cells. The neurons involved in creating the memory have a new structure and function as a result of their response to the experience. Your brain lays down a new physical circuit, and you retain that physical circuit—that memory—forever. Simply put: **The act of creating a memory changes your brain.**

We exercise quite a bit of control over this shaping of our brains. For instance, practicing a kind of activity or behavior strengthens the effectiveness of connections, reinforcing the circuit of the memory, and the brain's structure is altered. A gymnast's cerebellum, the area of the brain that has to do with balance and the fine control of movement, enlarges the more she practices.

Of course, the way we respond to stimulation from the outside world depends on a host of factors, including our own individual genetic makeup, hormonal levels, our sensory apparatus, and previous experiences. But we can actually change our brains. So even if we are different, we must tease out those differences, because we can learn from one another at the most fundamental level possible.

What We Know—And What We Don't

To begin this book, I'd like to present you with an overview of the science as we currently understand it, via true-or-false statements that come from questions I've been asked at lectures and by my patients. As you read, I'd like to remind you that while there do seem to be gender-specific ways of thinking, remembering, and experiencing emotion, those differences do not necessarily connote superiority. Dr. Kandel's groundbreaking research assures us that our brains aren't set in stone, even if our sex is. If we learn from each other, then these differences become opportunities, not divisions.

True or False: Sex is determined by our biology.

True *and* false. Although our sex is determined at the moment of our conception, and we stay that sex for the rest of our lives, we actually become *more or less* female or male over the course of our lives. Let's take a look at how this happens.

The sex chromosome contributed by our fathers pushes us to form male or female sex organs. Those organs, in turn, release hormones that cause dramatic and sex-specific changes to every organ and tissue in our bodies—including the brain—and program them to respond in sex-specific ways down the line. Varying levels of hormones over the course of our lives continue the process of sexing us.

In other words, our genes set us up for the sex we'll be, and our hormones salt the stew. The complex interaction between these two factors—especially during specific windows when their levels drop or surge as they do during puberty and menopause—make the two sexes different and each of us different from one another as well.

Nature is only part of the explanation for the differences between us. In fact, one of the thorniest challenges faced by those of us who study gender differences is teasing out which differences are due to the genetic and hormonal components of our biology and which are the result of "nurture," or how we're conditioned and shaped by our environment.

Society certainly believes men and women are different and expects sex-specific behavior from us. Even when children are young, parents encourage sons and daughters to do quite different kinds of activities, and in fact, boys and girls seem to enjoy quite different things.

These very disparate paradigms of what it means to be male or female provoke important questions about the difference between the sexes. How many of the differences between us are the result of the gender roles that the society of the time imposes? Are our sex-specific talents, temperament, and world view inescapably hardwired into our central nervous system? Or is our sexually stereotyped behavior choreographed by our culture's expectations of us?

Some of the differences between men and women are hardwired. But as soon as we're born, the environment works in powerful ways to interact with, and even change, our hardwiring to shape the way we act and interface with others. The idea that our experiences can change our brains means that the strands of conditioning and biology are more closely intertwined than we'd even thought. Treating your daughter like she's a girl may make her *more* so. The brain is never "done," but continues to grow and change as long as we provide it with inspiration.

True or False: There are significant differences between the brains of men and women.

True. It seems self-evident that men and women would have different brains—after all, what could be more fundamental about us than whether we're male or female? And yet, for most of medical history, doctors and scientists assumed that all the organs of men and women were the same, except for those directly involved in reproduction. Research suggesting otherwise is very new: Scientists first made the observation that there were differences in the physical structure of the brains of female and male rats a little more than three decades ago. It has now been confirmed that this is true not only in other species with two sexes, like songbirds and monkeys, but in our own as well: **The anatomy of the brain and *how it works* are different in men and women.**

True or False: The brain has a sex at birth.

True. Our sex is fixed and immutable—and not just at birth, but from the very moment of conception. That sex has implications for all the systems in our bodies, including our brains.

But in a sense, this is a trick question, because while we are undeniably and indelibly male or female from the very beginning, there are a variety of factors that contribute to the process by which we acquire our sex over the course of our lives. So, although you're always male or female, other factors are working on you at specific stages throughout your life to make you more or less that way.

What are those factors? Our genes are the unique cellular blueprint that makes us who we are, including our sex: The sex chromosome we get from our fathers at conception determines which sex organs we'll develop. An X chromosome from Dad means the baby will have two Xs and develop into a female. A Y chromosome means that there will be an XY complement, creating a boy. The sex organs we develop, in turn, release sex-specific hormones, which continue the process not only in the uterus but also during certain windows of time throughout life—puberty and menopause, for example—when hormone levels change precipitously. Those hormones also turn certain genes on or off, which further influences the sex-specific functions of our tissues, which is why more than one teenage girl has cursed her mother for the size (large or small) of her new breasts.

These genes are also why hormone levels vary from person to person. Those hormone levels affect our behavior. Individuals with high testosterone levels, for instance, are bolder, more aggressive, and more focused on a single goal. They smile less, have a higher libido, and are more likely to engage in extramarital sex.

There's one more factor influencing our sex—our experiences. A striking example of this is the conduct of some of the female soldiers at Abu Ghraib, the American-run prison in Iraq. Many of us were shocked—not just by the brutalities these women meted out, but at the discovery that women were just as capable of acts of humiliation and savagery as men. Clearly, experience is an important factor in modifying behavior.

True or False: Men's brains are bigger.

True. Whenever I lecture on this subject, nothing gets a more outraged response than this simple biological truth: Men's brains are bigger than those of women and weigh 10 percent more.

But size isn't everything. Women have more gray matter in certain parts of their brains and more intricate and extensive communications between brain cells than men, particularly in the frontal cortex. This is the area involved in judgment and decision making: the "executive center" of the brain. Some scientists think that this relatively more intricate system of neuronal interconnections explains why women's brains have a higher rate of blood flow. In fact, smaller brains may be more efficient. Ounce for ounce, women get more brain bang for the buck, possibly because of the greater degree of connectivity between cells.

And while it is true that male fetuses have more brain cells than female ones do, this may be the reason boys have more developmental defects than girls; it may require more energy to keep these larger brains in tip-top shape. It takes a lot of energy to drive a brain, especially a baby's brain, which has twice the number of working connections between cells as an adult's does. Boys, with their bigger brains, have significantly lower heart rates and lower body temperatures than girls; just when they need the energy to support their bigger brains, they fall behind! A higher number of boys have developmental disorders that become apparent in early childhood, such as mental retardation, expressive and receptive language disorders, stuttering, and autism; the energy deficit may explain why.

True or False: Women are better at multitasking, while men are better when concentrating on a single task from beginning to completion.

True. Ruben Gur, PhD, and Raquel Gur, MD, PhD, at the University of Pennsylvania in Philadelphia, measured blood flow and activity in men's and women's brains, and they found repeatedly that women use more parts of their brains when given a wide variety of verbal and spatial tasks. They believe that this may contribute to women's ability to focus on a number of different things at one time.

A new study has raised an important question: Women may be better at multitasking, but is multitasking really the most efficient way to work? Newer research shows that switching back and forth from one task to another takes precious seconds of reevaluation, and those seconds add up. As the researchers point out, in the best-case scenario, this makes you only slightly less efficient—but in the case of someone talking on a cell phone and driving, that fraction of a second may make the difference between life and death.

The conclusion I personally have come to is this: Multitasking is certainly helpful when you don't have any options, when your assistant is out sick or when you're trying to put dinner on the table while at the same time making sure your children are entertained and safe. But I find that when I need to concentrate on writing, it's helpful for me to turn off my phone and my e-mail program, with its constant "new mail" alerts, so that I can better and more purely concentrate on the task at hand.

True or False: The effects of our sex hormones (such as estrogen and testosterone) are restricted to the reproductive system.

False. There are two interesting things about hormones. The first is how *many* hormones play a role in sexing us—not just the sex hormones, as you might think, but others, like the ones we release when we're under stress.

The second is how many systems these hormones affect. Yes, estrogen is responsible for menstrual periods, but did you know that it also has a profound effect on the way women learn, think, and remember? For instance, estrogen may be one of the keys to the earlier questions about the differences between schizophrenia in men and women. Here's a more pedestrian example: I tell patients with young girls to keep an eye on their daughters' sneakers. The hormonal changes that announce puberty and bring on a girl's first menstrual period will cause a sudden surge in her growth and a leap in her shoe size as well.

All of the hormones in the body have far-reaching effects, which is why it's so important to take note when differing levels of them are found in men and women.

True or False: Boys and girls develop on different schedules.

True. One of the most important ways in which our brains are shaped is not through growth, but the programmed *death* of a large number—about half—of the neurons originally produced as the brain forms. This pruning process goes on from the final month of pregnancy and continues long after birth. Synapses, or connections between cells, that don't get reinforced by stimulation from the outside world atrophy and eventually disappear. The connections that are stimulated grow stronger and become permanent. You have to use it, or you lose it, and practice makes perfect.

It's a mysteriously wasteful process. Why don't we simply make what we need to begin with? I like to think that we're choosing the neurons that function optimally, like choosing the prettiest and healthiest flowers out of a bunch for a bouquet.

This brain tailoring process is part of what makes us unique: Our experiences—the stimulation we're exposed to, or protected from— have a very real impact on who we become. If we don't have appropriate input during these times, the systems can be impaired forever, and there are all too many examples of abused and neglected children who are cut off from interaction during crucial developmental windows and will never develop normal language skills as a result. Less tragically, it's what makes the differences between siblings and even identical twins who carry the same genetic information.

New information also tells us that how and when this brain tailoring occurs between the ages of 6 and 17 is different for boys and girls. There are major differences in *when* boys and girls prune and expand the connections in their brains, and in which areas they tend, as well as in the numbers of connections between the two halves of the brain in boys and girls. The hormones that surge during puberty (testosterone in boys, estrogen in girls) play a major role in these processes, as they have very different effects on brain function. These hormonal differences may be the reason for the different pace of development in pubescent boys and girls.

True or False: We treat boys and girls differently.

True. Of course, the society and culture in which we raise boys and girls has a tremendous impact on their outcomes. A landmark study done in the seventies showed that women tended to coo at babies dressed in pink jumpsuits, while men tossed those in blue up into the air. People tend to talk to girls, while they encourage boys to play with mechanical toys and objects, often from a very young age. In fact, this research leaves us unable to tell what comes first. Do the sex-specific innate areas of the brain make one sex function differently from the other? Or is it the impact of gender-specific behavior, induced by the societal roles we are asked to play? Gender bias may be even more important than we once thought, if the structure of our brains is in play.

True or False: There's no difference in the ways that men and women solve spatial problems.

False. There is evidence that men and women solve spatial problems differently. For example, precisely how men and women find their way through new and even familiar environments was tested in an interesting experiment done in Canada using a virtual reality maze. Not only did men and women activate completely different areas of their brains to negotiate the space, but they used *different strategies* to find the exit. Women used landmarks to guide them, while men used what was called "Euclidian information" to place themselves within the structure and navigate through it.

The researchers wondered whether the two sexes could use either strategy equally well and simply chose one over the other for reasons that weren't understood. They found that each performed less well when using the methods of the opposite sex, and they concluded that there is a real sex-specific difference in the way spatial problems are solved.

Apparently, in both animals and humans, the right brain houses the material we need to navigate our way through both familiar and new environments. It's risky business to relate the number or size of areas that are activated in response to a specific challenge to the success of how well the individual meets the challenge. But it is interesting to know that while both sexes activated part of the right brain, men used part of the left brain as well to do spatial tasks, which women didn't.

Men excel in their ability to imagine, for example, how a figure would appear if rotated in a space of two or three dimensions. Success with problems in advanced mathematics correlates with our ability to understand and manipulate three-dimensional relationships. Kerrin Christiansen and Rainer Knussmann from the University of Hamburg in Germany showed that higher testosterone levels in men correlated with men's enhanced spatial ability. However, they also found that those levels corresponded with their *diminished* ability for verbal expression—an area in which women excel.

There's excellent evidence that this spatial ability is hardwired into the human brain at birth and is the result of the sex-specific hormones we secrete during development. Baby girls who have an adrenal condition called congenital adrenal hyperplasia, or CAH, suffer from a buildup of masculinizing hormones as a result. These girls can appear very masculine (the enlarged clitoris of such a girl may be mistaken for a penis at birth), prefer roughhouse play, and are more likely to be sexually attracted to women than females without the disorder. They also have a better ability to solve spatial problems than unaffected females.

More evidence comes from studies of twins. Baby girls placed near a male fetus in utero seem to benefit from the additional boost of testosterone to which their brothers expose them: They have enhanced ability, for example, to solve three-dimensional problems compared with their singleton sisters.

Does this mean, as has so often been claimed, that boys and men are better at math? Maybe not. A 1990 study by psychologist Janet Hyde, PhD, looked at math ability in adolescent girls and boys and found that while boys did score better, the difference was in a mere few percentage points, not a significant majority. She did find, however, that there were more males at both extremes of the spectrum—the very high end of competence and at the lowest. Again, it's hard to extrapolate much of relevance there without more research. Most of all, it's impossible with what we know at the present time to decide how much ability people can cultivate by virtue of good teaching.

If girls are "worse" at math, it may have something to do with their socialization. Girls who took a math test believing that the test contained a gender bias (that they'd do worse, simply because they were girls) did worse than those who were told no such thing. In addition, girls in single-sex educational environments tend to do better in math than those in coed classes, perhaps because the implicit comparison with boys is removed.

Cultural stereotyping and discrimination are too subtle, insidious, and entrenched for us to dismiss them, even in supposedly gender-neutral, bias-free surroundings. For instance, did you have a female math or science mentor when you were growing up? I was lucky enough to get tremendous encouragement (and a wealth of medical knowledge) from a world-class researcher and doctor who happened to be a woman, but I know that I was privileged. An older doctor I know once joked that she first met a female doctor on the eve of her med school graduation—herself! This is changing; the women in science I know take a great deal of pride in extending a hand to their younger counterparts, but the overall question of whether young girls and women get the same opportunities in mathematics and the sciences is still a troublesome one.

Question: Why Has It Taken Us so Long to Study the Differences between Men and Women?

One of the very first questions I get when I'm lecturing about the implications of the sex differences between men and women is, "Why are we only just learning about this now?"

Because, for much of the time that we've been doing real medical research, we haven't studied women, we've studied only men.

But why?

It's a good question, and one that deserves a real answer. At all levels of scientific investigation, researchers believed that males were easier and better study subjects than women. They weren't wrong. Studying women is more complicated than studying men, and, in medical research, a "complication" translates to "expense." Men aren't subject to the same hormonal fluctuations over the course of the month that women are. Those fluctuations, which affect many of the body's systems, introduce variables that need to be taken into account when tabulating results. For instance, body temperature, a baseline measurement, rises in women at ovulation. Normal variations like these, which don't appear in men, can impact results.

It's also harder to do any kind of medical testing on women of childbearing age. Certain medications and techniques simply aren't appropriate because they may compromise fetal development—particularly in the very early stages (before a woman even knows she's pregnant)—or interfere with a woman's ability to conceive at all. And a pregnancy can throw a monkey wrench into collecting data for a long study. Too many changes take place over the course of a pregnancy for that person to remain a stable medical subject, even if what we're testing is safe.

It's still difficult to do the work we need to do to know what the differences are between women and men. It's difficult because women are more complicated test subjects and because it's difficult to get funding for research into this fascinating area. It's my hope that continued inquiry—driven by men and women—will illuminate some of these differences and that this new awareness will provide us with the strategies we need to move forward.

In the chapters to come, we'll look at some of the ways that men and women are different, and how those differences complicate and enervate the relationships we're in with one another. As the song says, the very beginning is a very good place to start, so in the next chapter, we'll explore what happens when two people meet and fall in love.

2

May I Have
This Dance?

What Attracts Us to One Another
and How We Fall in Love

Nothing is more mysterious to me than the alchemy that brings two people together, and I've discovered that it's as mysterious to the scientists who study this subject as it is to the rest of us. As Harvard's Daniel D. Federman, MD, put it, "The final aspect of sexuality, the choice of partners, is virtually terra incognita." What is the science behind what we find attractive about one another? What are the strategies we use to get to know one another a little bit better?

Many researchers believe that women search for partners who can provide emotional and financial security—in other words, someone who will be a good parent and a good provider. Men, on the other hand, are looking for someone who is young and healthy enough to reproduce; indeed, many of the physical characteristics that men find most attractive in women are ones that connote youth and good health.

These perceptions have been reinforced by studies, such as the massive, cross-cultural study done by Dr. David Buss, professor in psychology at the University of Texas at Austin, which found that men were seeking young, physically attractive partners, while women were looking for economically advantaged mates. From an evolutionary point of view, it makes perfect sense.

But one of the fabulous things about living in this new century is the fact that we're not exclusively driven by these evolutionary imperatives—in large part, because our environments and our opportunities have changed so dramatically and so quickly over the past 60 years.

First of all, the production of offspring isn't the only reason that men and women get together. We want love, sex, warmth, companionship, fun—any number of things from one another. In fact, in societies rich in material goods (like ours), personal pleasure is at least as important a driving force in the choices we make as having and successfully raising children.

Second, I believe the qualities we search for in a mate are changing as our roles in society change. As women's opportunities for education and career expand, so can the characteristics she seeks in a mate. A woman who makes her own living and can comfortably support herself and her children isn't dependent on finding a good provider. By the same token, an older man who has channeled his creative energy into his business, but wants intelligent company for dinner and a fun and fulfilling sex life, isn't limited to just the young and nubile.

We're dating longer and marrying later, which gives us more of an opportunity to have and learn from our experiences, and as we know, what we experience actually changes our brains. Chances are good that a bride walking down the aisle today has "kissed a lot of frogs" on her way to the altar. In the process, her definition of Mister Right may well have changed, from her very handsome but emotionally unavailable college boyfriend to the short, funny, smart, and kind man whose hand she now takes in marriage because he better serves her particular needs.

It is believed that many courtship rituals evolved so that females could assess the suitability of a potential mate. As Charles Darwin said about the species he studied, "Females are most excited by, or prefer pairing with, the more ornamented males, or those which are the best songsters, or play the best antics." It's sobering to realize that humans make our romantic decisions based on much the same grounds!

It's Not What We Say, But What We *Do*

Despite the vast numbers of sonnets and songs penned in an effort to attract the attention of a beloved, scientists believe that courtship between humans happens predominantly on a nonverbal level.

Hey, Good-Lookin'

Physical appearance is, of course, one of the very first things we notice about one another. A male bird's beautiful, brightly colored plumage intrigues prospective mates. The same is true of humans. I recently tried to persuade a good friend that charm and charisma were the things that men eventually and ultimately responded to in a woman. "The first thing we notice," he replied, without missing a beat, "is how she looks. If we don't think she's attractive, we never even get to the charm and charisma."

A study done in 1990 showed that women favored men with large eyes, prominent cheekbones, a large chin, and a big smile. The researchers who did the study said that these features indicated "sexual maturity and dominance." These characteristics are indicative of high levels of testosterone, which shapes the larger size and sharper contours of the male face. (Estrogen, on the other hand, is responsible for the round softness of women's faces and the extra fat in their cheeks and lips.) On some primal level, women found these very "masculine" facial characteristics attractive. Women were most attracted to men who seemed sociable, approachable, and of high social status. They also gave high marks to expensive or elegant clothing; apparently, it's not just birds who like beautiful plumage.

Men, on the other hand, look for features that signify good health: regular features, a good complexion, and a good body. (It will perhaps interest you to learn that—as you dreaded in junior high school— while large breast size does influence sexual attractiveness, it does not carry a lot of weight in mate selection.)

Another interesting observation: People choose mates with physical characteristics similar to their own (hence couples really do look alike, as dogs resemble their owners).

Are we all just fundamental narcissists? I think it's more likely that after a lifetime of looking at ourselves in the mirror, our features and coloring seem "right" to us somehow. Maybe we choose the genetic material closest to our own, in an "If it ain't broke, don't fix it" paradigm.

Don't Limit Your Options!

A few months ago, I ran into a friend of mine, out for a walk with a male companion. The first thing that struck me about my friend's date was that he wasn't very handsome or well dressed. But the next things I noticed about him were his lively and intelligent eyes and the laugh lines around them. In the brief chat the three of us had on that street corner, he impressed me with how charming he was and how attentive he was to my friend. I walked away very pleased that she had found someone so appropriate.

My friend is not a shallow person, but she clearly felt uncomfortable with the social pressure of dating someone who didn't look the way she thought her escort should. She undoubtedly knew, without my saying a word, what I had thought when I first laid eyes on him, and I wish that we were close enough for me to tell her what I thought next. I felt very sad for her when I heard they had broken up, and even sadder when she showed up at a dinner party we were both attending with a stunningly handsome man who treated her as if she were a not-very-intelligent child of 5.

I'm no soothsayer, but I feel sure that my friend had a much better chance of happiness and laughter with the man she was with when I ran into her that day, even if she had to stoop a little to kiss him. And yet, women like her throw away great relationships all the time (or nip them in the bud before they even begin) because the man is "inappropriate" in some way—too short, not handsome enough, not well dressed enough, not intellectual or wealthy enough, the wrong race or religion, too young or too old.

The social pressure isn't limited to women; in fact, it may be worse for men. (There is a play right now on Broadway by Neil LaBute, painfully titled *Fat Pig,* about a man who, because of social pressure, is incapable of dating an overweight woman with whom he has a terrific connection. Needless to say, it ends badly, as all the classic tragedies do.)

If there's one thing I know as a doctor, it's that you can't control other people's behavior. But if you take one piece of advice from this book, I hope it's this: Throw away all your old preconceived notions about what Prince Charming is going to look like, how old he will be, what he will wear, or what's he's going to talk about at parties; it will make you much more likely to find him.

A Token of My Affection

Psychologist Linda Mealey, PhD, of the College of Saint Benedict in Minnesota demonstrates how many of the mating behaviors of animals echo our own behavior, particularly in the use of carefully chosen objects to entice the female.

For example, the bowerbirds of Australia collect brightly colored objects that they display for the female's consideration in a cleared area called a court. Some select only blue decorations; others collect the plumage of a rare bird of paradise. These gifts offer a female the chance to assess how good the male is at accruing resources and how well he will provide.

In many cases, the quality of these gifts—which are not really so different from the diamond solitaire that traditionally accompanies a marriage proposal—can weigh heavily in a female bowerbird's decision about whether or not to mate with a given male. We don't have to look too far to find parallels in human society as well. Indeed, many women are likely to favor the man with the resources to buy her that house in the country or the status car and jewelry she's always longed for.

Ask any woman what's most important in a prospective mate and 9 times out of 10 she'll say "a sense of humor." It's my theory that this is another, more modern way of sniffing out his ability to accrue resources. A sense of humor takes intelligence and indicates charm: Surely these are far more useful skills in earning a good living in today's world than big pectoral muscles or a square jaw!

50 Is the New 40!

Another way, of course, for a female—bird or human—to assess a mate's suitability is by giving him a test, ostensibly to determine what kind of a protector he'll be. Jared Diamond, PhD, of the David Geffen

School of Medicine at UCLA, describes the incredibly complicated bower of the yellow-fronted gardener bowerbird of New Guinea, made of literally hundreds of different objects and including leaves that weigh half as much as the bird itself! He remarks, "It is as if a woman were to put her suitors through a sewing contest, chess tournament, boxing match, and weight-lifting contest before going to bed with the winner."

Here's something from the bowerbird research that I thought was interesting: Females of every age were attracted to the most heavily decorated bowers, but only older females watched the male's show in its entirety. Younger females lost their hearts to appearances—the males who'd built the best nests—but the older birds mated with the males who gave the most accomplished performance, which may be the best indicator of good genes.

I'm pleased to report that the traditionally male way of courting is expanding to include both sexes, as women become more financially and socially powerful. I'm not ordinarily all that interested in celebrity gossip, but my ears did perk up a few years ago during a wave of articles describing a rash of May-December romances in Hollywood. Hardly news, you might think; after all, Charlie Chaplin was 56 when he married the 17-year-old Oona O'Neill in 1943. But these more recent stories were all about older *women* in relationships with considerably younger men. In all of the cases, the women in the relationships were more powerful, with more money and clout, than their chosen mates.

I think this has a lot to do with the fact that men and women peak sexually at different times. Although men are fertile much longer than women, they are in their sexual prime in their late teens and 20s, and impotence begins to be an issue at about 40. In contrast, women can enjoy sexual exchanges for decades longer and sometimes even more after menopause, when the worries of conception aren't a factor anymore. It's my theory that, as the pursuit of sexual pleasure as an end unto itself becomes more acceptable for women, older women are seeking out the partners they need to make that happen: younger men!

I tell my patients and friends that they shouldn't be afraid to "date out of the box." Age is incidental these days: The old paradigm that women can only marry, love, and have children with someone 2 to 10 years older is truly out of date. This is of special relevance for older women, whose sexual needs can't be met by a same-aged or older male. Fifty is the new 40!

The Sniff Test

In fact, attraction between people may be taking place at a level even more subtle than clothing choice or facial appearance. There's considerable evidence to suggest that we're drawn together by our sense of smell.

It's not surprising that Proust's madeleine prompted five volumes of memoirs. The smell of a cookie reminded him of his childhood and was the beginning of his remembrances of things past. When we look at scans of the brain as the subject is smelling, the areas of the brain that deal with mood, emotion, and memory light up. Different smells have different effects. If you believe the aromatherapists, lavender is soothing and sleep-promoting, while pine energizes. The smell of a loved man's armpits has been demonstrated to reduce tension in women (although that probably won't be an option at your spa anytime soon).

Women do have a better sense of smell than men, possibly because of our estrogen levels. Recently, there has been an uptick in the number of female sommeliers and beverage managers at some of New York's best restaurants. A friend of mine who knows wine says the women put the men to shame during the high-level tastings he attends.

When we smell someone new, we may be gathering data about a mate's potential suitability. Under the soap, shampoo, and perfumes we adorn ourselves with, every person has a unique and individual scent, like a fingerprint. Newborn babies, just a few days old, can differentiate between genders on smell alone and will express a preference for the smell of their mothers over anyone else. The US Defense Department is considering developing technologies that would be able to identify people based on their signature smells. Scientists call this unique smell our *odor type,* and many believe that it plays a significant role in whom we find attractive.

"Opposites Attract"

There may be more to the Felix-and-Oscar truism than we know. In fact, researchers believe that one of the things we seek out in someone else's smell is that it be *unlike our own.*

There's evidence that your odor type is linked to genes that determine your immunity. People of different odor types seem to have different immunological resistance—so that someone with Odortype A might be immune to three different strains of flu, while a B is immune to three other different ones. Mating across odor types, then, is an evolutionary gambit to ensure that our babies have a wider band of immunity than we and our mates do on our own. (It may also be a way to make sure that we don't accidentally breed with a family member.)

Sending a Message

A pheromone is a chemical signal that one party sends to another to influence its behavior. Animals decode the signal by smell, using small collections of tissue in their noses called the vomeronasal organ (VMO).

For instance, male mice release a pheromone that will block the pregnancy of a female mouse that has been impregnated by another male. Researchers believe that pheromones are why the menstrual cycles of women who live together (in a college dormitory, for instance) become synchronized, and why men's beards grow bushy and full when they're in the company of women, but straggly when they're in the company of other men or are alone.

One of the principal roles of these signals in animals is sexual attraction. (The two Greek roots that make up the word pheromone itself mean *transfer* and *excitement*.) There's some controversy among researchers as to whether these chemical signals are one of the tricks that humans have at our disposal to attract each other. Babies have well-developed VMOs, but they may atrophy as they grow up. I think there's enough to merit further research on this topic; after all, even if we don't have this organ anymore, that doesn't mean we don't communicate via pheromones.

I once heard a woman say that she could tell everything she needed to know about a man from their first kiss. She might have been right! Kissing gives us the chance to get a great big "taste" of the chemical signals the other person is sending—and to transfer some excitement while we're at it. Increasing our exposure to the other person's pheromones certainly would explain how courtship behaviors escalate—why we move from conversation to close conversation to dancing to kissing, for instance. If we're trading chemical messengers, then the closer we get to the object of our attraction, the more "information" about them we receive.

New research, done by Dr. Ivanka Savic and colleagues at the Karolinska Institute in Stockholm, Sweden, would seem to prove not just that humans do have pheromones, but that they do play a significant role in attraction. Dr. Savic's work shows that homosexual and heterosexual men's hypothalmuses respond differently to two odors (a testosterone derivative in men's sweat and an estrogen derivative in women's urine) that may be involved in sexual arousal. Gay men respond in the same way that women do, perhaps suggesting that the way this part of the brain functions in this context is dictated by sexual orientation, not biological sex.

One of the fascinating things about pheromones is that they work not just on each other, but on ourselves; the pheromones we release may heighten our own sexual attraction and interest. I'm not the first one to wonder if they're responsible for the heightened attraction that everyone else seems to feel toward you when you're in the first flush of an affair. I remember running out for provisions after meeting a wonderful man, and it seemed that every single man I passed on the street "picked up the scent" and looked at me with interest, although I hadn't taken my customary care with hair and makeup.

So physical features, odor types, and pheromones may all play a part in the dance of attraction that takes place between a man and a woman in the first stages of courtship. Unfortunately, these are, for the most part, things you cannot control. (I certainly do not recommend the "pheromone perfumes" that were all the rage a few years ago. There is scant scientific evidence to suggest that they do anything.) But as you'll see in the next section, it's not all chance. In fact, women especially play a very important role in how the courtship proceeds, and they can use this role to determine what they need from their suitors and how well he fits those needs.

Women Are in the Driver's Seat

Even in these liberated times, it's hard to find a woman who has taken the initiative and asked a man she was attracted to out on a date.

Thankfully, this does seem to be changing. My youngest patients seem nonchalant about asking their teenage friends to the movies. But I still encounter tremendous resistance when I suggest it as an option to a friend or patient who's pining for some oblivious man. The blame may lie with the culture. Women are still told, often as soon as we begin to date, that men don't like "aggressive" women, so we tend to wait for him to call.

Given how passive we still consider the woman's role to be in courtship, it's surprising to learn from researchers who study flirting and courtship behavior how much the female really "directs" the action.

The evolutionary reason for this is fairly obvious: Mating decisions have much more serious consequences for the female, who will be the one who carries, gives birth to, and raises her baby to maturity—a process that takes a long time in human beings. Since it is so time-consuming for her, and since she has a limited number of opportunities to do it (as opposed to men, who can father countless offspring, given the chance)—it behooves a woman to make a good choice!

Women are not such shrinking violets after all. The first *overt* approach is usually made by the man—but only after a series of subtle signals sent by the woman. For instance, one researcher found that (both in the lab and in a bar) conversation between a man and a woman began only after a glance from the woman. Another discovered in field studies at singles' bars that the woman was responsible for courtship initiation about 70 percent of the time. But the signals women send are so subtle that it seems—to everyone involved—as if the man is really making "the first move."

A Dance as Old as Time

Waiting for a friend at a bar, Ellen sees a handsome stranger at the other side of the room. They make very brief eye contact; almost immediately, she lowers her eyes and looks away. She looks back, and they make eye contact again. This time, she doesn't look away until he does, and if we could attach electrodes to both of their chests, we'd discover that they're now breathing in synchrony.

Ellen lets her eyes wander up and down the handsome stranger's body. She cocks her heads, pouts a little, flips her hair, and a smile plays across her lips as he approaches the seat next to her at the bar. For someone who's being approached, Ellen seems to be doing a lot of the work!

Ellen's behavior, as he strikes up a conversation, continues to flatter him and encourage his intentions. She smiles widely and often, nodding, and leaning toward him and laughing. She makes a lot of gestures and touches his arm often. She touches herself, bringing attention to her hips and breasts, and applies a dab of lip gloss.

The same thing is happening—down to the very gestures used—in the bar next door and in one three-quarters of the way around the world. Ellen and the handsome stranger may simply tell their grandchildren it was love at first sight, but what was going on in the first moments of their courtship was actually a remarkably predictable sequence of events. ✎

What are the signals that women give men to let them know that we're interested—or that we're not? Researchers have put together a literal catalog of behaviors, including looks, pouting, flipping of hair, smiling, teasing, and laughing. (See "A Dance as Old as Time" above for more information on how women telegraph their availability.) Posture is important, as is the frequency with which we touch our conversational partner. We, of course, call these gestures flirting, but we may not realize how potent they are; in fact, the role of these nonverbal gestures is so powerful that the trained observers could use the frequency and strength of them to determine how a particular seduction would go.

For me, the most compelling discovery of that study was this: These gestures were *more important* in determining how the courtship progressed than physical attractiveness.

I found this research fascinating—it certainly changed the way I look at flirtatious couples and how I flirt myself—and very empowering. Newer research shows that women also give nonverbal cues designed to escalate or slow the pace of courtship, or to stop it altogether. The idea that we can control the pace at which courtship occurs gives us the space and time we need to determine our needs, and whether or not the man we're flirting with will satisfy those needs.

Women Determine *Whether* Courtship Will Continue, and the Pace at Which It Does.

As I always tell the patients who use their annual checkups as opportunities to bring me up to date on their love lives, it helps to know what you want. Everyone has a picture in their mind of their perfect mate, but does that picture jibe with what you *really* want from a life-partner? Are you looking for someone to settle down with and have children? Or a gorgeous hunk with bedroom eyes? Will you want to stay home to raise children, requiring someone else's financial support, or will you go back to your job after a short period of time and therefore need his domestic support more than his paycheck?

The most successful relationships I know of take place between people who sensibly looked for a complement in their life partner, not a "perfect match." And yet many of us get caught up in a hunt for a fantasy lover, one we think will go with our lifestyles just as our handbags accessorize our shoes. One of my patients described what she was looking for in a man. When she was done, I practically laughed out loud: She'd just described herself! The qualities she'd listed were things she thought she wanted, not things she *needed*—because those were things she could supply herself. The man she ended up happily married to is a complement to her, not a match. He supplies those things that she cannot.

The perfect partner isn't a fashion ornament, designed to say something about you to the world. I hear a lot of women, especially successful ones, say that they won't consider a man who makes less money than they do. Ridiculous! One of the most successful marriages I know of is one in which the woman makes considerably more than her husband; she's a dynamite real estate salesperson, and he trades in rare books. (Although the value of what they sell is quite different, they both deal in luxury markets, so she helps him find clients, and he does the same for her.) She accounts for the majority of their household income, but since both parties are fine with that, it's not an issue between them. Don't keep track of who earns more money; it's irrelevant to happiness as long as the bills are paid.

What Happens When "It" Happens: Falling in Love

Your heart beats uncontrollably. You check your e-mail obsessively to see if there's a new message; when there is, you parse every single word for hidden meanings and carry a copy with you so you can experience the delirious joy of seeing his words wherever you are. Everything about him is perfect, from his sense of humor to his upper lip. You stay up all night together, talking and making love—and yet float through your obligations the next day as if you'd eaten three squares and gotten a sensible 8 hours of sleep.

What's wrong with you? Nothing—or nothing a doctor can help you with, anyway. You're in love.

The Supremes famously asked, "Why do fools fall in love?" I can answer that question (as can anyone who's been there): It feels terrific! It's not often in life that we're presented with such delicious sensations, and it's not hard to see why so many of us lose our heads when we're bitten by this bug. In fact, anthropologist Helen Fisher, the author of *Why We Love: The Nature and Chemistry of Romantic Love,* believes that romantic love is not just an emotional state, but a motivational one, as fundamental to our survival as hunger or thirst, because it propels us to make connections with one another. We fall in love because it feels good, and the future of our species depends on that good feeling.

Fisher's theory that love is a biological drive made instant sense to me—partially because I have happily experienced the very compelling and uncontrollable sensation of falling in love, but also because I have gone through periods of my life without it. The idea that we are propelled by our biology to fall in love explains why living without romantic love can be so terribly painful.

In a book about differences, I hope you'll find this next piece of news refreshing: Love is one area where men and women become very much alike, if only for a period of time. Romantic love seems to erase the differences between us, and, as you'll see, that's physiologically as well as psychologically true. It's not accidental that men and women find themselves working together more synergistically and organically during this magical time than any other. It's a way of strengthening the relationships during the fragile newborn phase, to ensure that they mature into the next one. I believe that there is much that we can learn from this time of uncommon closeness, to sustain us when the differences between us are more marked.

This Is Your Brain;
This Is Your Brain in Love

I'm a romantic at heart, but that doesn't stop me from telling you that the key to love in humans has much to do with the interaction of a few important chemicals.

British neurobiologists Andreas Bartels and Semir Zeki, watched the brain activity of men and women when they were shown the picture of someone they had recently fallen in love with. The researchers were startled to see how clear and distinct—and universally shared—the brain patterns were. Regardless of whatever differences (sex included) the participants might have had, when they fell in love and looked at pictures of those people, their brains looked like the brains of other people in love.

The researchers saw that one of the parts of the brain that was strongly activated has a lot of receptors for dopamine, the "feel-good" neurotransmitter associated with motivation and pleasure. This is one of the reasons that love feels good. Other activities that trigger dopamine release include cigarette smoking and the use of cocaine. The drug comparison, incidentally, is explicit: In the British study, there was a great deal of overlap between the activity of the brain in love and the brain on euphoria-inducing drugs. The toleration for sleeplessness, lack of appetite, feelings of exhilaration and focus—these all characterize the first phase of an infatuation, but they're also very similar to what happens when you do a line of cocaine.

When something feels good, it's only natural to want to do it again, so it's not surprising that dopamine is also strongly associated with addiction. For some people with fewer dopamine receptors in the communication center of their brains, simply wanting to do a

pleasurable activity again eventually becomes wanting to do that activity all the time. The result is someone with a disturbance in the
pleasure-seeking part of the brain—a chronic overeater, for instance,
or a drug addict. I think it's fascinating that the very same chemical
is at work when we find ourselves in the throes of a crush. Perhaps
"love junkies," those people who compulsively chase new infatuations—often at the cost of their other relationships—are literally addicted to love?

The implications are very important, especially since scientists believe that there's a genetic component to other addiction disorders.
Both obesity and drug and alcohol abuse run in families, suggesting
that the disturbance in the pleasure-seeking portions of the brain that
causes these addictions can be, at least in part, inherited. Maybe scientists will eventually discover the gene array that powers those people
who seem doomed to desperately passionate (and inevitably short-
lived) serial romances.

The fact that drugs use the very same receptors that your brain
needs to feel love may shed light on one of the most devastating aspects
of drug abuse. Families are often shocked to their very cores by the way
a drug addict will turn against the family, without seeming to give a
second thought to things they would otherwise never consider. "There
must be some mistake. Marla would *never* sell Great-grandmother's an-
tique jewelry," her desperate family members say. But Marla in the
throes of her addiction is a radically different Marla, and *that* Marla
would—and has—sold heirlooms for a fix. The fact that drugs and love
use the same pathways may be part of the reason why drug addicts find
it so easy to turn their backs on loved ones and family and choose the
drugs instead. In a sense, the drug crowds out the emotional capacity
for love. It is certainly true that dopamine, whether drug- or infatuation-
induced, can cloud your judgment.

A Natural High

When we fall in love, our brains modulate the release of two other chemicals that may be responsible for many of the emotions we associate with the early phases of an infatuation.

The first is phenyethylamine (PEA), a natural amphetamine that elevates our moods. (In fact, it's the release of PEA that triggers dopamine.) PEA speeds the connections between cells—one of the reasons you're so very clear-thinking, despite the fact that you stayed up all night talking and haven't eaten in days. (The French call those wonderful, sleepless evenings "white nights.")

PEA is also strongly associated with pleasure; it's one of the chemicals released when we eat chocolate. You often hear women say that a particularly decadent chocolate dessert is "better than sex," but have you ever heard someone say that it's "better than love"?

This strong stimulant is also part of the reason you feel so jumpy in the first weeks of a romance (often unpleasantly so), and it can make you feel sick to your stomach—a sensation that's easily mistaken for butterflies when you see your beau. (Dr. Bartels, the author of the previously mentioned British brain scan study, also points out that one of the four distinct areas of the brain that was highlighted when participants looked at photos of loved ones is also responsible for our perception of our stomachs, which may be another connection between infatuation and butterflies.)

The other chemical that your brain releases when you're in love is norepinephrine, or noradrenaline. Usually associated with a state of emergency, this neurotransmitter is the one responsible for your elevated blood pressure and heart rate, your sweaty palms, and your intense focus on your beloved. Although it's also partially responsible for the euphoria you feel—which is why norepinephrine is a major player in some of the major antidepressant and antianxiety medications on the market today—it's also released during periods of high anxiety and anger.

When you fall in love, levels of another chemical called serotonin may be *reduced*—often to a level as low as someone with obsessive-compulsive disorder. This is a little surprising, considering that reduced serotonin levels are strongly associated with depression; the most popular antidepressants (such as Prozac) enhance the transmission of this chemical. But researchers have been quick to point out that there are very real similarities between someone who's smitten and someone with an obsessive pathology. If you've ever had to listen to a friend's repetitive cataloging of her new paramour's wonderful personality traits, you'd see how that's true. It's the low levels of this particular brain chemical that give us that laser focus and compulsive interest level.

Low serotonin levels may also be why, when you're not speeding along on love's terrific high, you're insecure and susceptible to the terrifying bogeymen that tell you he'll never call again and that he's all wrong for you and that you've just made a tremendous fool of yourself by manufacturing this whole inane schoolgirl infatuation in your head.

So what we think of as the first flush of romantic love is in fact the result of a chemical cocktail, one that replicates many of the sensations of illegal drug use. The brain continues to operate as the command and control center for the length of time that we're smitten.

Crazy in Love

No matter how pleasurable falling in love might seem, it is unquestionably an altered state. The roller coaster ride our hormones take us on in the first few months or years of a relationship eventually evens out. In the meantime, however, you might as well resign yourself to behaving in a way that's quite unlike yourself.

For instance, our brains in love may blind us to our new partners' faults—literally. The normal faculties that you bring to assessing another person in a social situation ("She looks tired" or "His laugh is terribly grating") are largely silenced when looking at your new lover. Those neural circuits simply don't fire.

This love blindness obviously promotes bonding. If we noticed all of each other's warts and bad habits in the first few weeks, the majority of relationships wouldn't make it through the first month. But it is sobering to think of the trick our brains are playing on us, and it certainly explains those times when you've looked back at an infatuation and wondered what you could possibly have been thinking when you fell head over heels. In fact, you *weren't* thinking—or the critical judgment part of your brain wasn't, anyway.

More Alike Than Different

As the song says, love will keep us together. And that's precisely what Donatella Marazziti, a professor of psychiatry at the University of Pisa in Italy, found when she looked at testosterone levels of a small group of men and women in love.

When we're searching for a partner, our sexual appetites are restricted only by attraction; the field is wide open. But when you fall in love, your sexual focus becomes tunnel vision; you have eyes for one person only, and it seems positively inconceivable that you'll ever allow anyone else to touch you again. A male friend of mine, known for his playboy ways, tells me that he knows it's "the real thing" only when other attractive women fail to distract him. And when it comes to that one person, you may find yourself astonished (even if you ordinarily have a healthy sexual appetite) by the intensity of the passion you feel and how much you want to express that passion sexually. Love can make you feel like you're 18 again, in more ways than one.

Dr. Marazziti may be able to explain why our lust is so powerful and so single-mindedly focused on the object of our affection in the early stages of love. Testosterone is the primary hormone that drives sexual appetite in both sexes, and both sexes show an elevation in testosterone levels during periods when they're sexually active. But in Dr. Marazziti's study, the men had *lower* than normal levels of testosterone, while the women's levels were higher than normal. In other words, (hormonally speaking, anyway) men and women met in the middle.

Falling in Love Made Men and Women *More Like Each Other*

Dr. Marazziti speculates that this similarity in hormone levels helps to solidify relationships in their shaky early stages by erasing differences. Women with higher testosterone levels are more aggressive and assertive and have a greater sex drive than usual. Men with lower testosterone are less aggressive and less libidinous, making it more likely that they'll keep their eye on the mate right in front of them. The changes in their hormonal levels allow the two sexes to narrow the gap that might otherwise exist between them, which increases the likelihood that they'll bond together successfully.

Blaise Pascal, the 17th century French mathemitician, said, "The heart has its reasons which reason does not know." I heard a scientist say recently that our first mistake was trying to separate "the mind" from "the brain"; his point was that all our behavior is governed by molecules in our brains. It occurs to me that we should extend his comment to include the heart. Is the apparently incomprehensible way we fall in love (and with whom we fall in love) simply a disturbance in our neurons and neurotransmitters? Possibly. But that hardly makes it any less delicious.

Now that we've gotten you into bed, let's talk about what happens once you're there.

Can We Leave the Lights On? Sex Differences in the Bedroom

In Plato's *Symposium,* Aristophanes tells us that the first humans were both male and female. They were very beautiful, insufferably pleased with themselves, and, above all, self-sufficient (as many of us surely would be if there was never the need to woo and keep a mate!). According to the story, these early humans were so enchanted with their own perfection that they planned to attack and conquer the gods themselves. Zeus, king of the gods, decided to punish their arrogance by dividing each of them into two sexes: male and female.

The newly separated humans were so lonely for their missing halves that they found themselves unable to work or function, eventually dying off from sheer longing. When he saw what he'd done, Zeus had second thoughts and consulted Apollo, the god of medicine, to devise a method to reunite the two sexes, if only temporarily. Apollo obliged with the ingenious idea of sexual intercourse. (Evidently, the sensation of boundaries dissolving between people during a passionate encounter has a mythological basis, if not a scientific one.)

Poetic as this may be, and as mystical as sex may seem to well-suited lovers, the reality—what actually happens between two people in bed—may in fact be quite different. Instead of finding our long-lost missing half, many people find sex unsatisfying, uncomfortable, or undesirable. To judge from popular magazines and television, you'd think the sheets were on fire, but the statistics (and my patients) tell us otherwise.

The sad statistic is that sexual dysfunction (low desire, difficulty in becoming aroused and/or reaching orgasm, and painful intercourse) affects 43 percent of women and 31 percent of men. You've probably noticed the proliferation of medications designed to address sexual dysfunction.

Doctors tend to reduce sex to a very specific and well-regulated cascade of events, requiring the coordinated activity of a cast of thousands of nerves, blood vessels, and chemicals. Sometimes this viewpoint can result in oversimplification: "Low libido? Here's a prescription for Viagra or a testosterone patch." In defense of my colleagues, many patients want an instant fix for boredom, pain, or anxiety and prefer a pill to the difficult business of sorting out what's really wrong and what to do about it. It's much easier to believe that faulty hormone levels are to blame for lackluster performance in the bedroom than other, more difficult problems requiring time, sacrifice, or a difficult conversation.

But clearly, hormones aren't the whole answer. If the wags are right, the brain is the largest erogenous zone (especially for women), and we'll need a great deal more research on how that organ operates to ensure a satisfactory sex life. Dissecting sex may not be very appetizing, but I'd like to know more about how everything works when patients tell me what's going wrong in the bedroom and ask me what to do about it.

As you've probably noticed in your own life, there are some stark differences between men and women in this area. Are the sexual differences between men and women the result of differences in our brains? I can't tell you because we don't know. But what we do know about the differences between the way men and women experience sex may help us improve our relationships, not to mention our general well-being. Because no matter how you try to tamp it down, ignore it, chase it, avoid it, fear it, enjoy it—and whether you revel in anonymity or surround it with the trappings of romantic love—sex occupies an elemental, perhaps even primal, force in our lives.

What Turns Us On?

Researchers are just beginning to use new ways of looking at the brain in action, including PET scanning (which measures increases in blood flow in various parts of the brain), to see exactly what's happening during sex. There are only a few published studies. All of them involve very small numbers of patients, and—tellingly—all have been done only on men.

One study from Holland traced brain activity during stimulation and ejaculation in eight men brought to climax in the laboratory by their female partners. As with some of the other activities we'll discuss in this book, like talking and listening, men seem to use one side of their brain rather than both during sex. In these subjects, who were all right-handed, most of the places in the upper parts of the brain that lit up during sex were on the right side. This peculiarity of men's brains during sex helps to explain why sexual dysfunction is higher in men who have had strokes that involve the right side of the brain rather than in those who've had damage on the left.

One of the most fascinating results these researchers found may solve the question that begins this section (and that every woman has heard at least once in her life): Can we leave the lights on? Men do like to watch. Visual stimulation plays a strong role in their sexual arousal, a more significant one than it does for women.

There are many studies confirming this, but I don't think we have to look much further than the $57 billion worldwide pornography industry for proof. Pornography is an overwhelmingly male pleasure, and I think there are now enough discreet avenues for women to purchase pornography anonymously to rule out social stigma as a reason there aren't more women using it. Women are consuming and enjoying more pornography than ever before, but the fact is that the lion's share is bought by and looked at by men.

This difference between us may be hardwired. Although the subjects of the study in Holland had their eyes closed, the part of the cortex that processes and integrates visual images was active. The part of the cortex associated with memory-related imagery was also activated; the men may have used mental images to become aroused, specifically images that had turned them on before. They were stimulated by visual images, even though their eyes were closed!

In fact, different parts of our brains "turn on" when we're turned on. An interesting study that looked at the areas of the brain that were activated when men and women viewed erotic films showed that the patterns of activity were different for the two sexes. Men in particular had increased action in the hypothalamus, which plays an essential role in sexual arousal. We have known for years that the hypothalamus has gender-specific structural differences, but these investigators saw that it behaves differently in response to pornography in men and women. This structural difference may explain men's greater interest in visual stimulation.

I know that many women are upset by their partners' use of pornography; I hear about it a great deal from my patients. I advise them (and you) not to take it personally. It tends not to have anything to do with you or how he feels about you, and the research would seem to confirm my suspicions. If you still think it's a statement about your own attractiveness, remember that the sight of *you* doing erotic things is also a turn-on; offering that instead may be a perfectly suitable substitute.

There is another interesting difference between men and women regarding sexual arousal. Thirty years of research has established that gay men are aroused by images of men, and heterosexual men by those of women. Women are a little more complicated. Dr. J. Michael Bailey, professor and chair of psychology at Northwestern University in Evanston, Illinois, has shown that women—whether straight or gay—have a bisexual arousal pattern and enjoy both male and female erotica. This study used an interesting control group to rule out the possibility that the differences they found were really a measurement issue (men's arousal is more easily and visibly determined than women's). They tested postoperative transsexuals, people who had begun life as men, but who had undergone surgery to construct vaginas. Their psychological and genital arousal matched those of men. If they were heterosexual, they were stimulated by female erotica; if not, they were more aroused by male films.

Insert Tab A Into . . . Uh, Wait a Minute

One of the most revolutionary shifts that has taken place since we've begun to ask what's different about women and men sexually is in our understanding of *the sequence* in which it all happens. Clinicians have traditionally divided the sexual experience into distinct phases, each one leading into the next, and sexual dysfunction as a problem with one or several steps in the cascade.

This turns out to be simplistic—and in the case of women, downright wrong. In the sixties, sex researchers Masters and Johnson described a sequence that began with a state of physiological arousal (erection in men and increased genital blood flow and muscle tension for women) triggered by any sexual stimulus. The arousal stage is followed by mounting and then by increasingly urgent sexual tension that culminates in orgasm.

And that's pretty much the way it works—for men. For instance, men almost always (although not invariably) report subjective feelings of arousal when they have an erection. But newer research shows that even when women are apparently *physically* sexually aroused, with clitoral engorgement and a lubricated vagina, they may not *feel* sexually aroused—a disconnect that simply doesn't exist for a man. Just as important, women can feel interested in sex and aroused, even with very little or no vaginal lubrication. Helen Singer Kaplan, MD, PhD, further tweaked Masters and Johnson's model by making desire—the subjective experience of lust or hunger for a sexual experience—the inevitable predecessor of arousal, followed by orgasm. But here again, while this sequence may be true of most men, it may *not* be true for women.

Innovative new research shows that the truth may be closer to one proposed by a doctor more than a hundred years ago—Elizabeth Blackwell, MD, who in 1849 became the first woman to earn a medical degree in the United States. For most of the five decades that Dr. Blackwell practiced medicine, attitudes toward sexuality were, well, Victorian. There was almost no sexual education—for either sex—before marriage, and there was a widely held belief that women were asexual. The situation was compounded by a best-selling marriage manual at the time, which counseled the regular exercise of a man's "privileges of marriage" (read: rape).

Dr. Blackwell believed that the proponents of these untruths suffered a "misconception of the meaning of human sex in its entirety." In her eloquent reprimand, Dr. Blackwell reminded husbands that wives are indeed capable of sexual feeling and passion, but that a woman's arousal is dependent on a "mental element" and "a delight in kiss and caress." That "mental element" is the "highest and mightiest form of human sexual passion" and distinguishes human love from animal sex.

Certainly, women are more capable of enjoying sex without love than Dr. Blackwell may have suspected, but there is unquestionably a grain of truth in what she wrote. A century later, Rosemary Basson, FRCP, suggested that the biological drive to have sex is not nearly as strong in females as is that to nourish and protect offspring and that women go to bed as much out of a desire for an intimate connection to another human being as for simple lust. She further proposed that the sexual exchange for women doesn't begin with sexual arousal, but with a desire for *increased emotional intimacy.* It is this desire that persuades women to engage in sex.

Indeed, the mind-body connection in women as regards sex is complex and fascinating. Sex researcher Dr. Sandra R. Leiblum describes women for whom the physical aspects of sexual arousal (genital and breast engorgement and sensitivity) can persist for hours or even days without desire—or *any experience of sexual enjoyment, satisfaction, or pleasure at all.* Sometimes a woman may need multiple orgasms to resolve these physiologic signs of arousal. Susceptible women can even be physically aroused by stimuli that aren't ordinarily considered to be sexual at all. Women who suffer these kinds of experiences of prolonged and unwelcome physiologic arousal without any sense of sexual interest or pleasure experience them as concerning and unwelcome.

I find the implications of this research fascinating. Being turned on, apparently, isn't the be-all and end-all for women, which is why it will pay to be cautious as we invest time and energy in finding a Viagra equivalent for women. This research shows why a pharmaceutical solution like this will be helpful for those who have difficulty with the biological manifestations of arousal—and how it will leave women with other issues out in the cold.

One thing seems clear: Pure lust seems to be more important for men than it is for women. Many, many studies—of how much women and men think about sex, what they think about, the variety of the things (and people) they think about, how often they masturbate, how often they want to have sex, how long they're willing to go without, what they're willing to give up to get it, and how often they initiate it—show that men have a stronger sex drive than women.

And the feelings women have for their partners do have an important impact on whether or not they experience desire for their partners. From what I can tell, anger seems to be the most effective neutralizer of psychological arousal for a female, *even though she may be physiologically aroused.* I don't know how many of my women patients have told me they simply can't go to bed with a lover with whom they're angry. In 30 years of practice, I've never heard that from a man—possibly because men don't remember disagreements as long or in as much detail as women do.

Foreplay, Please

Women's enhanced enjoyment of intimacy may be why some of the most satisfactory episodes my women patients and friends have described to me begin hours before consummation—over a leisurely dinner, perhaps, on the dance floor, or with a bouquet sent before their date even arrives.

It may also explain the importance women accord to foreplay. It's well worth the effort, gentlemen! If men's visual sense is more developed than that of women, it's fair to say that all the other senses are more finely tuned in females, especially smell, taste, and touch. And it's not just dinner and dancing, but the physical stimulation itself.

For many women, having pleasant genital sensations may *precede* and indeed, ignite desire, not the other way around. Many women need a partner's initiating maneuvers to experience desire. Only after they feel an increasing sense of intimacy, sparked by their lover's touch, do they feel desire and begin to respond. With this, we may have the answer—in hormonal form—to the age-old question of why women seem to need more foreplay than men do.

For Women, Arousal and Desire Can Exist Simultaneously and Reinforce One Another

This research gives rise to what might be the most controversial piece of advice in this book, but it's one I believe in, especially given what we know about the difference in the way men and women experience the sequence of arousal.

The advice is this: If you're feeling lackluster about sex, allow yourself to be seduced. (It goes without saying that this requires a sensitive and responsive partner—one who will stop, without fail or question, if this experiment fails.) The word *seduction* comes from the Latin, meaning to lead one away from oneself. Physical touch—unfortunately, it has to be someone else's touch!—stimulates the production of a very powerful and intoxicating hormone called oxytocin, also called the love hormone because of the feelings it engenders. It's this hormone that prompts female rats to crouch and raise their hindquarters high in the air, which signals they are receptive to interested males.

Oxytocin seems to stimulate sexual desire in both sexes, probably because it simulates the production of testosterone, which is strongly linked to sexual appetite in both men and women. It's also one of the factors that contributes to the ease with which women become physiologically aroused. Levels of this hormone increase both during arousal and after orgasm. It even raises sperm counts! The

For Men Only:

There's an old joke: God is handing out His very last gifts to the new couple in Paradise. He announces: "I've only got two things left. Who wants to be able to urinate standing up?" Adam jumps forward and takes that one. God turns to Eve and says, "That leaves you with the multiple orgasms."

After an orgasm and ejaculation, men have a period of time in which they aren't, and can't be, aroused. Women, on the other hand, have a unique capacity for multiple climaxes without having to go back to square one and begin the cycle all over again; they simply remain at a high peak of sexual arousal and may orgasm several times in succession.

Great, right? Well, yes. And no. This brings us to another feature of women's experience that has not been fully explored or explained. If a woman's partner prolongs that sequence of orgasms, she may ultimately find the experience not only unsatisfying but unpleasant. It's a little like eating more chocolate cake than you really wanted; the first bite was terrific, and maybe even the second piece was great, but by the fourth or fifth, it's really not what you want to be doing anymore.

Perhaps the lesson here is that being a truly great lover means knowing how to please your partner—and knowing when to leave well enough alone! ◟

fact that oxytocin's effects are particularly enhanced by estrogen may be a reason women are more sensitive to touch than men are. Sex itself increases oxytocin production and probably creates the all-important "afterglow" of serenity and closeness that happens after orgasm. A fascinating effect of oxytocin is that it *impairs memory,* which is probably why lovemaking can wipe out the impact of an argument.

Satisfaction Guaranteed

If only! Very recently (probably because more women are talking about sex and more men are listening), researchers have added another essential ingredient to the mix: For women, *satisfaction* with a sexual exchange is an important element in the whole process. This research suggests a new criterion for defining sexual dysfunction in women: "personal distress," which acknowledges that at least in humans, sex can be deeply and profoundly unsatisfying—even when everything is apparently satisfactory, from arousal to orgasm.

Both men and women can experience orgasm without having a sense of sexual gratification. And there are women who don't always have to have an orgasm to feel sexually satisfied. Comfort, reassurance, tenderness, and a sense of being protected are as important—or more so—as an orgasm for these women. The word *intercourse* comes from the Latin words *inter currere*, meaning "to run between" or "to exchange something between two individuals." That always seemed to me to be the essence of the activity, and it seems to be borne out by this new research.

"Not Tonight, Dear. . . ." What Happens When Your Libido Flags

Mila is typical of many of my 40-something patients. When I ask her if she is sexually active, she looks down at her lap and says, "Not really."

Mila's not unusual. I have a number of patients in long-term relationships who tell me that they rarely (or never) sleep with their husbands (or anyone else) anymore. Sometimes my patients tell me that they're quite satisfied with their husband's friendship, or that the decision *not* to have sex has left them happier than they were when sex was an important factor in their relationships. If that's the case for both parties, then more power to them.

In many cases, though, the lack of sex in the relationship is a source of pain and stress. Often, the wife is disinterested, but concerned that her husband will begin looking somewhere else for gratification. Indeed, it does seem that when sex isn't happening in a relationship, it begins to happen outside of it.

My advice to Mila is simple: If it's not happening in your body, use your brain! We shroud sex with a kind of mystical aura, so that we feel quite helpless when sexual attraction comes upon us—and even more helpless when it departs. My female patients often approach me for a pill that will put them back on track, but I can usually determine whether the reason for their trouble is biological or not with a simple question: "How's sex on your vacations together?" If the answer is "fine," as it often is, then it's something about life at home that's getting in the way of having a happy and fulfilling sex life there. And if looking at the pool guy gets you as hot and bothered as a teenager, then the problem isn't with your libido.

It's not surprising. Life and its attendant stresses can be pretty unsexy sometimes. Cortisol, an important hormone produced by the adrenal gland, is called the stress hormone. It's meant to soothe the body's response to threat and mitigate the effects of stress. Unfortunately, it has a depressive effect on sexual interest and performance. So it's not surprising when sex suffers in marriages where both partners are stressed, whether about money, job security, the health of their children, homeland security, or the myriad other pressures that encroach upon our private time together.

But there's hope. If the brain is a woman's biggest erogenous zone, then we wield a tremendous amount of control over our libidos. Evidence of this is everywhere—even in clinical trials! A fascinating study done by Mary Lake Polan, MD, PhD, MPH, professor and chair of obstetrics and gynecology at UC Stanford, looked at a nutritional supplement called ArginMax, which contains a simple amino acid called L-arginine. Dr. Polan found that 62 percent of the women who took it reported greater satisfaction with their overall sex lives compared with 43 percent of the placebo group. I am very interested in her results—and not just because I'm curious about the effects of L-arginine on female sexuality. Read the results again: An astonishing 43 percent of the women in the placebo group saw improvement, even though they were taking a supposedly inert substance! If just *thinking* that your sex life might improve (and monitoring whether or not it does) actually increases sexual satisfaction, it goes to show that we can do a great deal indeed to re-energize our flagging libidos.

As we know, for women especially, sex is a process of getting engaged. First, ask yourself some questions. What is standing in the way of your libido? What creative solutions can you implement to remove the source of the problem? Fatigue and a lack of privacy are often the culprits when a family is young. If you find that you're too tired after the baby goes down at night, why not get cozy with one another during the weekend naps, and check e-mail or do the household chores you'd scheduled for that time later, when your energy level is lower. Trust me, I'm a doctor: Sex is more important than folding the laundry!

(Incidentally, most scientists seem to agree that a hormone called prolactin—particularly high in nursing mothers—inhibits sexuality, which may be why new mothers report decreased sexual desire compared to their prepregnancy states. Nursing is a wonderful experience, fulfilling in its own right, but it may help you and your partner to be mindful that doing so may be having a short-term effect on your sex drive.)

Get intimate: Many women tell me that problems in the bedroom arise when they don't feel intimate with their mates. Sometimes you have to make intimacy happen—and accept that this is a process that may take place over a couple of days. Go for a walk together or cuddle up and watch a movie. Ask him what's going on at work and tell him about the concerns of your own day. What would make you more re-laxed? Would a glass of wine help? A back or foot rub? Ask for what you want; as you probably have noticed, this is one scenario where your partner is pretty highly motivated.

Spice it up: Boredom and restlessness are also common culprits in long-standing relationships. They too can be alleviated by applying a little mental energy to the problem. What have you done in the past that you both enjoyed? Is there anything worth trying again (a trip, an erotic video or storybook, a sexual aid that's gone dusty under the bed from lack of use?) Does thinking about those times give you any ideas of other things you might try? Ask yourself what you can do to make your typical lovemaking session more novel and therefore more inter-esting to you.

Talk about it: Often, simply addressing the problem head-on can get the ball rolling in a more positive direction. A woman came in to me, complaining that her sex life with a longtime companion had lost its oomph. Both of them felt it, and she was concerned because it seemed like he'd been avoiding relations with her recently. I asked her, point-blank, what she liked and disliked about sex—and then advised her to go home and put the question to her lover.

She told me with some amusement later that his answer to the question surprised both of them. Apparently, he had been finding sex *tiring.* Both of them preferred him to be on top in the classic missionary position, but he wasn't as in shape as he had been and found the exer-tion overwhelming. They resolved to experiment with positions that put less strain on him, and he—motivated by sex as he could never have been motivated by high cholesterol, I was amused to note—began an exercise regimen to improve his aerobic fitness.

Explore HT: If you've found your libido falling off since you've gone through menopause, you may want to consider talking to your physician about hormone therapy (HT). Yes, there were some apparently damaging implications of the results from recent studies that show that HT in postmenopausal women can cause early and harmful effects in a small subset of the population. But not all women are at high risk, and for women who are not (your physician can tell you if you are or not), it's an option to consider.

The positive impact that HT has on a patient's sex life is one of those things that I've heard over and over from my patients, although it's simply not reported—or denied—in the literature. More than one specialist has said that "estrogens have little direct influence on sexual desire in either males or females," but I've heard differently from lots of women, both patients and friends, and from anthropologist Helen Fisher, who has studied sexual activity in humans quite extensively. One of my patients, an octogenarian who has taken HT since menopause, just celebrated the first anniversary of her very erotic relationship with her lover. She reported with glee, "Estrogen is the greatest thing in the world!"

It makes sense to me. Estrogen increases blood flow to organs, including the tissues in the pelvis and the perineum. This explains why some women become much more sexually aroused in the first trimester of pregnancy, when estrogen levels are rapidly rising, and I have heard from many women that they found it much easier to become aroused by erotic stimuli or fantasies once they started HT. Estrogen also appears to increase the ease with which they achieve orgasm and *increases the intensity of their orgasm.* At a recent conference, Dr. Fisher asked me: "Why don't they tell women estrogen improves orgasms?" It beats me!

Check your medications: I notice the difference between the importance men and women put on sex every single time I write a prescription for a medication. Men will ask about sexual side effects before my pen has touched my pad; I can't remember any female patient of

Help—It Hurts!

Sheri, a lovely woman in her 40s, had been referred to me by one of my oldest patients, after confessing that she had been experiencing a sensation of rawness and irritation in her genital area.

The burning pain made even walking difficult—and lovemaking with her adored husband totally unthinkable. Her previous doctor had "prescribed" a romantic vacation without the kids, but I wasn't convinced that Sheri's problem was in her head, particularly after talking to her about what seemed like a loving marriage without previous intimacy problems.

In fact, Sheri was suffering from a condition called vulvar vestibulitis, which may be caused by an inflammation of the pudendal nerve. The condition—notoriously difficult to treat, much less cure—may last for years, or come and go periodically. Thankfully, Sheri does experience long periods of dormancy, and I'm happy to report that she and her husband are just back from a romantic vacation—no thanks to her previous doctor.

Too many women's complaints of genital pain are dismissed as hysterical, or the result of a long-ago (and perhaps suppressed) negative sexual experience. In fact, a complaint of this type always merits further investigation. There are a number of physical causes for genital pain, and they're not uncommon—For example, a gynecologist can expect that about 15 percent of his patients will have vulvar vestibulitis like Sheri does.

It's not the only cause. Some postmenopausal women who are not on hormone therapy may experience a thinning and atrophying of the vaginal wall that makes lubrication impossible. The dry surface is then vulnerable to injury from penetration and friction. Another disorder, called vaginismus, is caused by an involuntary spasm of the outer third of the muscles of the vaginal wall, which makes penetration difficult or impossible.

There may indeed be connections formed during past experiences of sexual abuse or injury that cause these conditions, but that is really not known. Psychotherapy can be helpful in relieving them. Certainly more research is needed, but in the meantime, the least you can expect from your doctor is a referral to someone who may know more.

If you feel reluctance (or an inability) to have sex because of pain, find a doctor who will work with you to rule out a physical cause. ⌒

mine ever doing that. Many men complain within days that a medication is affecting their sexual performance, while women never even connect a lessening of libido or difficulty in achieving orgasm with the drugs they're prescribed.

In fact, some of the most commonly used medications do have sexual side effects. If you take any of the medications below, and believe that they're adversely affecting your sex life, talk to your doctor about lowering your dose or trying a similar medication with a different side-effect profile.

- **SSRIs:** Selective serotonin reuptake inhibitors such as fluoxetine (Prozac) depress libido and make orgasm hard to achieve. Women seem more affected than men. These medications may affect an area in the brain stem that communicates directly with nerves in the lumbosacral spinal cord (in the small of the back and the pelvic area) that are important in orgasms for both sexes.
- **Beta-blockers:** These medications, which are some of the most commonly used to treat high blood pressure in women, depress libido and sexual performance. Mysteriously, they're the first choice for many physicians in treating women (but not men) with high blood pressure. I've always ascribed this to the antianxiety effects that many beta-blockers also have. I think that doctors often assume that out-of-control emotional responses contribute significantly to hypertension in females. Beta-blockers often have names that end in "olol." Ask your doctor exactly what he's prescribing to treat your hypertension; there are many other choices besides a beta-blocker to bring your numbers under control.
- **Street drugs:** While low doses of cocaine, which enhances dopamine activity, enhance sexual pleasure and delay ejaculation, chronic use impairs sexual function. High doses prevent erection, as

cocaine constricts blood vessels. Heroin and other morphine-like drugs decrease sexual interest and competence in both sexes. Ecstasy (methylenedioxymethamphetamine, or MDMA) became popular among young people at nightclubs because it increases sociability and sexuality. Women should be especially careful with this one. At least in laboratory animals, estrogen increases the degree of excitement the drug produces, and females become much more stimulated than males.

As you've probably gathered, this chapter isn't meant to be a comprehensive overview of everything you can do to remedy what goes wrong in the bedroom. I simply want to bring your attention to a few simple facts that may have weighty implications on what happens between you and your partner, and to some commonsense ways to bridge the gap. There is a quantitative difference in the way men and women experience desire and the sexual act itself—differences that may very well be hardwired. We can use what little we know about those differences to positively affect the intimate interactions we have.

3

What Did You Say?

The Differences between How We Listen and What We Hear

"You never listen to me!"
"Have you even heard a word I've said?"
"Men just don't get it!"

In some ways, meeting one another and getting together are the easy parts. All too often, it's when we have to start really relating to one another—talking, listening, negotiating, and compromising—that the problems begin.

It seems that there is no bigger difference between men and women—and no difference that causes more friction—than the way we communicate with one another. Our difficulties in talking and listening to one another are the subject of countless books, daytime talk shows, jokes, and conversations between friends. With good reason: As all too many couples have discovered, the ability to communicate effectively can get two people through the worst parts of a relationship; without it, there is no relationship at all.

Whether you're making love or parenting or getting old together, the quality of that interaction is governed by the quality of your communication about it. Being able to talk—and perhaps more important, to listen—is positively fundamental. That's why this chapter, where we'll take a look at some of the basic differences in the way we hear and speak, and the next chapter, where I tell you what to do about it, are so important. They'll give you the tools you'll need to navigate whatever life throws your way.

Why Is It So Hard?

Men and women have so many of the same interests, and yet, I hear it over and over—from my friends, my patients, and yes, even myself: Sometimes talking to the men in our lives is like banging your head against a brick wall. They don't listen, or they're irritated at the things we say; they don't respond to our comments, and even when they do, they don't say the right things. I sometimes think it's a miracle we manage to live together as effectively as we do, given how hard it sometimes is to communicate with one another. Why the disconnect? And what can we do to repair it?

In fact, some of the difficulties that men and women have in communicating may have a biological basis. There's considerable scientific evidence to suggest that men hear, listen to, understand, and produce speech differently than women do.

How We Hear

We're actually born with a slight difference in our hearing apparatus. Newborn girls can process and interpret sounds better than same-age boys. This is the reason baby girls recognize sounds like their mothers' voices sooner than baby boys do. As far as we know right now, this doesn't translate into a difference in the way adult men and women hear. But it is interesting to note that there is a discrepancy in how well we hear right off the bat, as well as a difference in the systems in the brain that we use to decode what spoken language really means.

There's an old joke that men lose 50 percent of their hearing once they say "I do." In my experience, there's no ring required. Communication difficulties take place between fathers and daughters, brothers and sisters, and on one-night stands. Certainly, men's ability to process language and understand what's said to them begins to diminish as early as age 35, while women preserve this function until they're menopausal.

At that point, the playing field evens out a bit, with an interesting twist. A study published in the *Journal of Speech, Language, and Hearing Research* showed that women lose their ability to assess cues from the tone of someone's voice for a period of time after menopause. This is part of the cognitive dissonance that comes from an estrogen dip, the same dip that can also make it difficult for menopausal women to remember details and make decisions. Like those lapses, it has an impact on our ability to navigate the world. Tone, of course, adds essential information to our communications. It tells us when a comment is meant to be ironic, a joke, or just plain cruel. If you strip the loving, teasing vocal note out of even the most gentle jibe, it can sound harsh and hurtful. This tone deafness may explain the complaint I hear so often about perimenopausal women—"She takes everything I say the wrong way!"

There's some evidence that men, no matter what their age, actually process the information they hear differently than women do because of fundamental differences in their brains. In general, humans use the left part of the two symmetrical halves of our brains to produce language and understand speech, and the right for dealing with tasks that involve our physical position and other spatial relationships.

Some of the differences between men's and women's brains that may cause differences in the way we process and produce information include the following:

• Women have *more nerve cells* in the left half of the brain, the seat of our ability to process language.

In the brain, quantity of cells often does correlate with quality. In the brain of a gymnast, for instance, the part of the brain that controls balance and motor skills is larger than it is in other people, and the more she practices, the larger it gets.

• Women have a *greater degree of connectivity* between the two parts of the brain.

The thick network of fibers that connect the two halves of the brain, called the corpus callosum, is larger in women than it is in men. This may lead to greater traffic between the two halves of the brain in women. For example, men and women appear to process single words in a similar fashion, but when they're interpreting full sentences, men tend to use a single specific area in the brain, while women mobilize the same areas, *but in both sides.* A study at Indiana University in 2000 showed that women used an area of the brain just above the ears in both halves of their brains in listening to an excerpt from a John Grisham book, while men used the same region, but only on the left side.

I find the revelation that men and women actually use different systems to hear staggering—and one with many as-yet unexplored implications. If it is found that women and men actually process and decode what they hear differently, will it change the way we educate the two sexes? Advertise to them? Talk to one another? We can only imagine.

• Women have more dopamine in the part of the brain that controls language.

Nerve cells don't talk to each other by touching; they release chemical messengers called neurotransmitters, which are picked up and "read" by other nerve cells. Women have higher concentrations of the neurotransmitter called dopamine in the part of the brain responsible for language and memory skills. In other words, their cells have more messengers at their disposal, and more messengers means more information delivered more efficiently. Researchers believe that women score higher on tests of verbal learning than men, particularly if they are younger, in part because of this higher dopamine availability in their brains.

So women appear to use *more* of their brains—they have more cells, and they use a greater percentage, encompassing more areas—in listening to and in making speech. Does that necessarily mean that women are better at it? There are any number of studies to suggest that they are, but I prefer to think of it this way: The increased accessibility of some of these systems may make listening to, understanding, and producing speech *easier* for women.

Listening to—and decoding the meaning of—the spoken word is *easier* for women.

Facial Expressions: Worth a Thousand Words?

There's another, very significant difference between the way women and men "hear." We're very different in our sensitivity to facial expressions, tone of voice, and other manifestations of nonverbal nuance, or what researchers call "nonverbal leakage."

Men can identify straightforward emotions in others—like rage and aggression—sometimes even better than women can. They need to be able to assess aggression in other males so that they can speedily arrange a defense. But they don't score as high as women on the more subtle nonverbal cues that telegraph sadness and fear. Researchers believe that women's facility with understated cues is an evolutionary adaptation, designed to help women do the job of taking care of infants. A baby can't tell you that he's hungry or sick. To make sure he gets what he needs, his primary caretaker (usually the mother) must become very skilled at interpreting nonverbal cues, like a facial expression or the particular tone of a cry. (The word *infant* actually comes from the Latin for "without speech.")

People often comment on the seemingly uncanny ability of mothers to know what their babies want, based on what seems like scant information. Some of the best advice I got when I was a new mother was to pay attention to how I *reacted* when my baby cried. Indeed, a certain cry of real pain or fear would have me out of my chair before my conscious mind had even processed what I'd heard.

It seems that most women can tell if something is wrong with her child, a parent, or a spouse as soon as she lays eyes on them, while men can easily miss even the most blatant signs of distress. Women's skill in interpreting moods and emotions through nonverbal communication helps even once our children are out of infancy. We employ this skill-set at work, in our romantic relationships, and even in navigating casual encounters in a store or restaurant—not to mention deciphering the confusing signals sent by our adolescents!

Women Are Better at Identifying and Interpreting Nonverbal Cues, such as Tone of Voice and Facial Expression.

The difference in the way we respond to emotional expressions seems to be connected to a functional difference in the brain. One study showed that when women saw a fearful expression on someone's face, their amygdalas, the brain's warning center, the area that controls fear and our recognition of it, engaged more rapidly than men's did. Another brain study done in Japan showed that men and women used different parts of the brain to identify whether faces had happy, sad, or neutral expressions. The differences were greatest when the study participants were shown sad expressions, which women identified much more accurately than men.

I'm fascinated by additional research that suggests that our ability to interpret emotions on the faces of others depends on their sex. One small study from a very good laboratory used professional actors and actresses to display different emotions. In this study, men had a higher overall accuracy in identifying sad expressions, but they were far less accurate if the sadness was on a female face! Women were more accurate in identifying a wide range of emotions on male faces than they were with those in women's faces.

I think of women's ability to interpret a wide range of complex expressions as an "empathy advantage." In fact, Simon Baron-Cohen, PhD, offers a controversial theory to explain autism that hinges on just this difference. He speculates that our brains naturally lean toward one of two tendencies: the ability to understand systems or the ability to have an appropriate response to someone else's emotions. Men tend to be more interested in how things work, while women are more empathic. People suffering from autism, a childhood developmental disorder without a known cause or cure, are characterized by their detachment from other people and the physical environment and by their difficulties in communicating or relating emotionally to other people. Dr. Baron-Cohen believes that autistics have an "extreme male brain," potentially caused by exposure to high levels of testosterone in utero. Autism, then, takes the standard male lack of empathy to an extreme.

I am not entirely convinced. While I am not an expert in autism, I would hesitate to say that what these children suffer from is a lack of empathy. In fact, Temple Grandin, a well-known autistic scholar and writer, has used what I consider to be astonishing empathy—borne out of her experience as an autistic person—to improve the conditions of animals in the slaughterhouse and to reduce the amount of fear they feel as they approach death. In her case, it seems that autism has enriched her capacity for empathy, instead of numbing it. But Dr. Baron-Cohen's theory is a fascinating one, especially given that boys are three times more likely to suffer from autism than girls are.

What's Wrong with You?

Not surprisingly, the differences in men's and women's sensitivity to nonverbal cues can be the source of much conflict. You're sure that the emotions you're feeling must be as clear as the nose on your face, and yet he hardly seems to notice! Women are often frustrated by men's inabilities to "read" us; when we sulk, don't answer, cry, storm out of the room, or look hurt, we expect a response, but all too often, none is forthcoming. It's a very lonely feeling. "I'm not a mind reader," he says, exasperated, when you confront him with the evidence that he doesn't pay enough attention to your feelings.

In fact, blaming him for failing to read the nonverbal cues you're sending isn't really fair. It's not something at which he's innately accomplished! Blaming him for missing your cues is like playing hide and seek with someone who's gone home early. If your goal is effective communication, it pays to remember that the man you're talking to can't interpret your nonverbal signs and signals as well as you can read his. (Incidentally, I believe that women are sometimes *too* sensitive to the cues other people put out—to their own detriment. Your waiter may indeed be in a bad mood, but that shouldn't ruin your lunch.)

The interpretation of nonverbal cues is one of the areas where I think that the sexes have much to learn from one another. This is especially true for physicians. As the Nobel Laureate Bernard Lown has said, doctors must be especially "sensitive to the unshed tear, the skipped beat." One of my colleagues, one of the best diagnosticians I know, makes a conscious effort to listen not just to the answers patients give, but to the expressions on their faces and the tones of their voices. He is convinced that this has made him a better doctor, and he loves to tell stories of medical clues he unearthed simply by following up on a change in a patient's tone of voice or expression.

I know from my own experience that paying attention to the patient across the desk doesn't just involve listening: Watching is as (or more) important. For example, if I ask about a patient's child and she answers with an expression of sadness or anger—even if the verbal answer she gives me is neutral—I know that there's more there than meets the ear and that I'm one step closer to unearthing the cause of her chronic insomnia.

Of course, it isn't just the medical profession that would benefit from better and more active listening. And it's not just in our professional lives that we benefit from using *all* the information someone gives us to make a determination about their mental state. A father who pays attention to his child's body language as they approach his school may get important clues about his social life there; a woman who watches her lover's reaction to another woman's flirtation may get more from his physical response than she will in questioning him later.

Why Men Never Remember and Women Never Forget

There's some evidence (as the very title of this book suggests) that women have better memories than men do for the spoken word. Never is this more apparent than during an argument! During a disagreement, one of my partners—a lawyer—wryly asked me to "read back his last statement," as he would ask the court reporter during a trial. I could and did.

Women have a higher rate of blood flow to certain parts of the brain, including those that control language. This is one of the reasons researchers give for the overwhelming evidence that women have better immediate and delayed recall of the spoken word. Studies of brain blood flow in men and women instructed to remember stories and word lists confirm that when women commit a story to memory, there is enhanced blood flow to the area of the brain that acts to systematize and form concepts of what they are hearing. This makes it easier for the memory of the story to be "packaged," sliced and diced so that it can be efficiently stored and subsequently retrieved. Both sexes retained the information over long periods of time, showing that information *storage* was equally good for both sexes. But women scored higher than men on their ability to recall both stories and lists immediately after hearing them.

Another reason given for women's memory strengths is the higher concentration of the hormone estrogen. (Incidentally, men have estrogen too, but at lower concentrations. Testosterone, by the way, is an important precursor of estrogen. An enzyme called aromatase converts testosterone to estrogen within cells. Paradoxically, it's actually the higher intracellular concentrations of the "female" sex hormone estrogen in the male fetus's brain that masculinize his brain.) There is abundant evidence to show that estrogen activates more nerve cells, increases blood flow to certain areas of the brain, and increases the complexity of connections between nerve cells. Higher levels of it are associated with improved learning and memory, and this may be why women are better at these tasks.

Estrogen also plays a protective role in brain function, which is one of the reasons that men's brains atrophy more with aging. Hormone therapy (HT), which increases estrogen levels in postmenopausal women if given soon enough after menopause, restores and protects our ability to concentrate and to remember things.

Estrogen is also an element in a key finding: that women remember stressful events better than men do. This rang true to me the minute I came across it in the literature. For instance, one study of elderly men and women (the average age was 77) showed that even very elderly women had more intense feelings when remembering emotional experiences than the men did.

Here's why. Estrogen not only activates a larger field of neurons in women during an upsetting experience, meaning that they experience the stress more intensely, but it also prolongs the amount of time that the adrenal gland secretes the stress hormone cortisol—which happens to be a natural memory booster. That's why simply remembering an unpleasant incident can bring back the same terrible sadness and agitation that was experienced at the time.

Researchers speculate that there is an evolutionary basis for this. If women are the primary caretakers of their young, then it behooves them to remember potentially dangerous situations, like which plants are poisonous and which watering spots are already spoken for by animals with large teeth. Men have no such facility, for a similar evolutionary reason. If a man has perfect recall of how scared he felt during the last mammoth hunt, he'll be far less enthusiastic about going out this time which is not what you want when dinner depends on his fearlessness.

I think it comes as a tremendous surprise to many women that men don't remember the substance of our arguments, and I wouldn't be surprised if this in part explains the wildly disparate ways we sometimes characterize the arguments that take place between us. One of my patients took a vacation with her longtime boyfriend. They spent most of the time away discussing some of the major issues in their relationship. At the end of the trip, she told him she'd learned a lot and thought it improved her understanding of what was going wrong (and right) between them. He, on the other hand, told her he'd hated the hours they'd spent on the subject and had found the whole exercise pointless and even destructive.

Perhaps their conflicting memories of the vacation had something to do with their memories of the events. My patient could have mapped out a flowchart of issues raised, solutions proposed, and resolutions adopted, even months later. Her boyfriend, on the other hand, was considerably fuzzier on the specifics even hours afterward, and soon after stepping off the plane, he remembered only "fighting."

When Women's Memories Work against Us

"You're bringing up that again?!?"

The husband of my patient Bella came to her five years ago and confessed he was having an affair. Although he swears that he has been faithful since, that long-ago infidelity still pollutes every moment of her waking life. There's no pleasant afternoon spent together that isn't colored for her by the memory, and in every quarrel about unrelated issues, she manages to remind him of his perfidy.

I know why Bella's still so angry. She feels the betrayal as viscerally as she did when he told her about it. For him, it's over; for her, it's an ever-present specter spoiling their marriage. In some ways, the culture supports the "female" point of view on this subject: The currently-held common wisdom tells us that talking is good, while silence equals denial, and is therefore bad. Everything we read or see on television reassures us of how good it will feel to get things out in the open, to pursue closure, to remember always.

But is it really the best thing for us?

A fascinating article published in the *Journal of the American Medical Association* suggests that post-traumatic stress disorder, a psychiatric disorder that occurs after experiencing life-threatening events, is "just as much a problem in forgetting as remembering." The researchers conclude that it's "important for people to have privacy, to forget and not to have to talk." In a 2004 article in the *New Yorker,* Jerome Groopman, MD, explored whether recalling the details of a traumatic incident really helps to dispel its impact on the sufferer to determine how much (or how little) crisis counseling that revolves around reliving the incident actually helps. Recent data—regretfully available to us in the wake of the events of September 11, 2001—shows that forgetting or repressing the memory of the experiences might be much more helpful and conducive to real healing.

This may be an area in which women, with their tendency to return over and over to the scene of the crime, can learn from men. I might suggest that Bella take a page from her husband's book—for the sake of her mental health, not simply her marriage. Nothing will erase the fact that he was unfaithful to her, but for both of their sakes, she must make the decision to move on. When she told me about the affair and its effects on her, I naturally asked her why she stayed in the marriage at all. She immediately gave me five excellent reasons the relationship was still positive for her (incidentally, just doing that exercise alone can be very helpful indeed). I gently pointed out that since she had decided to stay, she needed to do her part to allow the marriage to heal, and they have since begun counseling.

What Are You Talking About? The Differences in How We Talk

We've just learned that women hear, and process what they hear, better than men do. But the ease with which women understand language extends to producing it as well. Women find verbal communication easier and have richer vocabularies than men. The vast majority of studies show that women outperform men in language tasks and produce speech more easily and fluently. To put it simply, we're better talkers.

This love of conversation, and our ability to use it to strengthen relationships, is one of the great joys of female friendship. My friends don't make points; they tell stories, and the ease with which we share conversation makes dinner or a drink together very enjoyable indeed. In the hands of women, a simple piece of parenting advice can turn into an extended and hilarious riff, while a report on office politics can make a corporate boardroom seem as shadowy and intrigue-filled as the court at Versailles.

Men, on the other hand, stick to the facts and often groan or roll their eyes when their wives launch into a long anecdote. One husband

I know actually mutters, "Here we go with another story!" as his wife begins one of her tales—no matter how amusing it seems to me.

Men classify the sort of talk that women are so good at as gossip, which connotes frivolity at best and malice at worst. This trivialization may comfort men when they suspect they are the targets of our tongues, but it's not really a fair assessment of the way women communicate. In fact, the stories women tell are an important way for women to exchange and remember information. This is a unique advantage, because it helps us to plot a safe and successful course through our lives—including the male-dominated workplace—just as it did when we were protecting our offspring from predators roaming the plains.

As much as I love the way my female friends talk, I'm also a fan of the way men handle spoken information. Unlike most women, they speak with terrific efficiency. I like my questions answered succinctly and directly, and when it's appropriate, I enjoy using that economy of expression myself. My poor secretary, who loves to repeat every detail of a message, finds this distressing and worries that I've missed something if I don't listen to every detail of what she has to tell me. When I'm really rushed, I interrupt her, which she ignores, simply increasing the volume until she's finished. I've learned to simply hear her out!

Of course, there are men who love a good gossip and women who don't, and I have certainly known men whose verbal facility was extraordinary. But either way, there is room for improvement in the way men and women talk to one another. Both parties have a great deal to gain from examining the differences in the way the two sexes talk, and *in adopting the best that both have to offer.* We can learn from one another, and in this particular area, we must.

Gift of Gab

Girls generally say their first words and speak in sentences earlier than boys do. Scientists at the National Institute of Child Health and Human Development studied 329 children in four separate studies and found that in the 2nd through 5th years of life, girls consistently outperformed boys in many aspects of language. They knew more words and had more expressive language than boys of the same age.

Some of this may be social—a result of the things that little girls are interested in and of the way we treat them, as opposed to their brothers. I still remember the remarkably rich chats I had with my 3-year-old daughter, and I suspect that some of them had to do with the activities she preferred. Dolls, for example, provoke a great deal of imaginative play, and there is much to say about what they and their stuffed animal compatriots are doing. Adults tend to roughhouse with baby boys or encourage them to play with toys like trucks—where beeps, rather than words, are the order of the day. Girls tend to spend more time with adults, especially their mothers. Even when I worked at night on a research paper that commanded all my attention, my daughter would play under my desk just to be near me. Girls also seem to play more in groups than boys. A particularly fascinating piece of research shows that girls in daycare centers receive more attention than boys and that their caretakers are more responsive and stimulating with girls than boys.

But at least some of the differences between the way men and women produce language may have to do with the way our gender-specific brains process and produce speech. There is a real difference in brain development between the sexes: Girls' brains mature earlier than those of boys, including the centers that generate speech. This may set girls up for verbal superiority during development. Other investigators found that the higher the testosterone levels in normal males, the less verbal ability they had. In a fascinating series of experiments, Sally Shaywitz, MD, at Yale University showed that when men and women did an identical word-rhyming task, men activated only one area in the left side of their brains, while women used the same part, but in both hemispheres rather than in just one.

This, as well as the greater degree of connectivity between brain cells in women, may also explain certain medical differences between the sexes. For instance, women recover speech more quickly and more successfully than men after a stroke. They also develop less of a speech deficit after a lesion that affects just one side of the brain. And boys have a higher incidence than girls of speech impediments, such as stuttering, and developmental language disorders like dyslexia.

The Body Language Divide

We've discussed the greater ease with which women interpret non-verbal cues, so it won't come as a surprise that women *use* more of them to communicate as well. Women tend to use facial expressions, verbal rhythm and tone, and physical gestures to convey information and emotion.

Why? Researchers believe that the explanation for this can be found in the nursery. Men are often irritated by the high-pitched cooing and exaggerated facial expressions women use when they're talking to babies. In fact, women—whether they know it or not—are doing it for a reason: Babies respond best to high-pitched voices repeating the same things over and over again and to "big" facial expressions, like wide smiles and wide-open eyes. Prioritizing clear communication with young children may also account for women's tendency to use their hands and bodies when they talk and for their greater tendency to touch their conversational partners.

Of course, a woman looks much different when she's talking to a toddler than she does when she's talking to another adult, but there does seem to be a carryover in style, even in adult discourse.

So women use more—and more varied—words than men do. They use more subtle and nuanced facial expressions than men do, smile more often, gesticulate more, make more direct eye contact, and are more likely to touch the person they're talking to.

Women Use More Physical Embellishment When They Talk

The bells and whistles that women add to their speech certainly does make for better communication with children, but I suspect that these superfluous ornaments of conversation can sometimes serve as a distraction when women are talking to men. When you're talking to a man, it pays to remember that a little goes a long way. It even distracts *me* when a woman's hands move around faster than the stream of words coming out of her mouth. Sometimes it's not just distracting, but downright irritating.

In certain circumstances—during an argument, for instance, or when I'm being interviewed on television—I restrict the number of gestures and facial expressions I use. Whatever additional nuance I might think I'm adding with those gestures and expressions is probably not reaching its target and, in fact, may be distracting my listener from my speech, which contains the real information I want to get across.

Men, however, might find it helpful to know that using some very basic and subtle gestures—a smile to acknowledge a witticism, a small nod in support and encouragement, narrowing the eyes to connote concentration—can go a long way when talking to a woman.

Two Worlds Collide

I was at a meeting of high-powered scientists a few months ago. During the lunch break, I surveyed the tables in the dining room to find a place to sit. Since I was busy reading the scientific literature about the sexually distinct brain to prepare for writing this book, I was naturally curious about what people at different tables were talking about.

I was fascinated to discover that where women were sitting together, the conversation was all about children, issues with aging parents, and apartment renovations—in short, domestic issues. Not a moment was used to discuss the provocative conversations we had all had earlier in the morning, when we were doing business together. The men, on the other hand, were talking about science and their jobs.

All of us in that room were professionals. The women had as much scientific prestige as the men (although there were fewer of us) and had taken part in a lively debate of the issues that had come up earlier in the day. But the focus of conversation at lunch was not only profoundly different for men and women, but homogeneous: No science crept into the females' exchanges, and no domestic notes into the males'.

I don't know why this is. Certainly it is some combination of our innate biology and the culture in which we are all raised. I know that my certitude about our innate biology is likely to raise some eyebrows, but having reviewed the evidence, I do feel confident that we are born with a brain that is specifically sexed due to a combination of our genetic code and the hormones we release and are exposed to *in utero*. As an example, we know that girls who are exposed to high levels of male sex hormones while they're still in the uterus are overwhelmingly likely to enjoy rough-and-tumble play—and to resist becoming parents later in life.

So I do think that the tremendous interest women have in their families is hardwired into the female brain. This hasn't, shouldn't, and won't stop us from doing other brilliant and fascinating things in our lives, but it does seem to affect the things we're interested in talking about. Whatever the causes, the result seems to be the same: Men and women put a different emphasis on different things.

Men and women prioritize different interests and have different ways of talking about them.

What Happens When We Fight?

Obviously, whatever difficulties we have in communicating are magnified exponentially when we fight. This explains why these interactions are so phenomenally frustrating (for both parties) and why they can be so damaging to our relationships.

But there may be some basic brain processes getting in the way of effective communication during a fight. First of all, activity in the amygdala, the part of the brain that controls emotion, increases. Activity in the frontal cortex, the part of the brain responsible for reasoning and problem solving, decreases. That's why you have difficulty sticking to your targeted points and making your argument coherently; you're talking from your heart and not your head. This may be even truer for women than for men who have had previous unpleasant experiences that are similar to the one they're currently having. Women's memories of these fights are more vivid and detailed than those of men.

What happens in your brain when you're angry is actually remarkably similar to what happens after an orgasm, and if I had a dime for everyone who'd said something they wish they hadn't after a passionate embrace, I'd be writing this from my own private island. In both situations, our brains are working *against us,* in a sense: Our emotions are high, and the logic center is dimmed. (I certainly wouldn't want to argue before the Supreme Court after really great sex—would you?)

And it's hard—for women in particular—to stop fighting, even when the issue that triggered the conflict has been resolved. In my experience, some of the most damaging things we say and do happen in the aftermath of a fight. When you experience extreme anger, a cascade of hormones are released into the bloodstream by the brain. One of the differences between women and men is that those levels return to normal much more slowly in women. Have you ever made up after a fight, only to realize that you're casting around for something else to be angry about? Everything's resolved, but you still feel angry—so you go agitatedly looking for something else to fuel the fire of the fight. If your boyfriend looks baffled, it's because those hormones are still buzzing around in your system, while his have long since returned to their resting state.

Another very common mistake in fights between couples is a tendency to mistake a man's specific disinterest for general disinterest. Let me explain. My friends Alex and Amy were planning to renovate their kitchen. Amy embraced the project, and soon the dining room table was buried under various fabric, tile, and paint samples. When she tried to elicit Alex's opinion, he seemed irritated and disinterested, so she accepted the responsibility and went ahead and ordered a style of cabinets she liked without checking with him first.

Alex was furious, and Amy was baffled. "I tried to get you to look at samples with me, and you kept saying they all looked the same!" I think the problem was that Alex wasn't comfortable with the level of detail to which Amy was exposing him.

(In my mind, it's not accidental that so much friction in relationships happens over decorating issues. In fact, there have been at least two studies—one done in Nepal, and one in England—demonstrating that women can name more colors than men can. There is a widely circulated joke on the Internet of "men's rules for women," and one of them is "We are like Microsoft Windows: We only recognize 16 colors. Peach is a fruit. So is melon. We have no idea what mauve is.")

Just because Alex didn't want to mull over the differences in 10 nearly identical pieces of stone for the countertop didn't mean he wanted to wash his hands of the whole renovation. He did want to have some input on the overall appearance of one of the most important rooms in their house, but he couldn't tolerate the level of detail that Amy could.

I would suggest to Amy that next time, she approach Alex with a few clearly differentiated choices. Stone or wood? Yellow or blue tile? I never go to one of my male colleagues with a complaint or problem without presenting him with at least two potential solutions. It's fun to mull over an infinite number of possibilities with my female friends, but I find that men give the best advice and analysis when they're choosing between a limited number of options.

Lost in Translation

Perhaps our difficulties in successfully talking to one another have to do with inaccuracies in the way we analyze the information we're given.

My patient Sarah described to me a conversation she'd had with her husband, Bill, as they were filling out an application together for a special gifted program for their son. In order to illustrate one of Liam's finer qualities, Sarah launched into an anecdote. Bill cut her off, wanting to "get to the point," which for him was how they could describe that quality in a sentence that would satisfy the application requirements. The interruption hurt Sarah's feelings, which irritated Bill. Needless to say, the application didn't get finished that night.

What we have here is pretty much textbook. Sarah answered a question with a story; Bill simply wanted to draw the shortest line between points A and B. Their inability to communicate properly left them each with hurt or bad feelings—and compromised their effectiveness as a team in completing the application.

It's humiliating to be interrupted, and there's really no excuse for it, no matter how pressing the deadline or how inappropriate the digression. That's something Bill is going to want to correct in the future. But when I did a little digging, I discovered that the interruption wasn't really what was bothering Sarah. It was her interpretation of what lay behind it. "Liam is his son too," she said. "What's more interesting and important to him than talking about our child?"

In my opinion, Sarah simply drew the wrong conclusion from the data. She thought Bill's disinterest in her anecdote betrayed a lack of interest in Liam. I'm not so convinced. In fact, I think Bill might have been acting in what he perceived to be Liam's best interests, by trying to finish the application. Rude? Yes. Disinterested? Probably not. But given Sarah's "translation" of Bill's behavior, of course she felt threatened and hurt!

We're More the Same As We Age

Don't worry; all is not lost. In fact, in the next chapter, I'm going to share some of the strategies I've discovered for overcoming the hurdles thrown up by the differences in the way we communicate. I strongly believe that we can learn to talk and listen to one another more effectively, and that we have a great deal to learn from one another, information that will help us to communicate better with everyone in our lives.

One of the most encouraging things I have read thus far about the differences in the way we listen is that the gap narrows as we age. For instance, in the study of elderly people mentioned earlier, although women may have felt more intense emotion when remembering important things that had happened to them in the past, researchers observed that there wasn't a significant difference in the number of facial expressions women used, compared with the men in the study. I feel confident saying that there would have been a difference in a study of younger people. Whether that means older women use fewer facial expressions than young women do, or older men use more than younger men, are questions for another time. What I take from it is that men and women become more alike in this area as they age.

I like to think that this greater degree of compatibility happens, not just because of the physiological changes that happen to us over time, but because we spend our lifetimes learning from one another and, in doing so, becoming more alike. Certainly, when we begin communicating better, one of the happy side benefits is the realization that our communication difficulties are not carved in stone. We can change the way we say things and the times we pick to say them, and we can monitor the response of our partners so we can continue to refine our approach. With a clearer understanding of the differences between us, we can plot a course around them, using tactics like the ones you'll find in the next chapter. It's my hope that gaining these insights earlier in our lives will save ourselves (and our partners) considerable grief.

4

Legato's Laws for Improving Communication between the Sexes

In the last chapter, we talked about how the differences between men and women manifest—and indeed, may be exacerbated—because of differences in the way we communicate. There is one constant truth, no matter what situation you find yourself confronting with your partner: Communication is the basic currency of relationships, so there is tremendous benefit in working to improve the flow of information between the two of you. A first step must necessarily be to find a lingua franca, a shared language that we can use when we need to exchange information with one another.

The pages that follow contain some strategies that I have found to be helpful when you are saying something to a man that you really, really want him to hear.

Put Him on Alert

Listening well may be harder for men than it is for women. As a result, I have found that it helps to let a man know when you're about to say something you really want him to hear—let him know it's coming! When you need to have a serious conversation with the man in your life, ask him to listen and let him know (in a gentle and uncritical way) that this is going to be what my friend Leslie calls a "look-me-in-the-eye conversation."

Ask Him for His Help.

The partners in our lives aren't required to act as our sounding boards. As I heard one comedian tell his wife, "This is a service I provide to you free of charge." There's a seed of truth there. Just because you share a bed doesn't necessarily mean you're obligated to listen to one another—although it certainly does make the relationship better when you do. But out of respect, why not be courteous and ask him to listen: "I'd like to get your input about something that's going on at work." You may be surprised how much attention this small courtesy gets you in return.

Pick a Time That's Convenient for *Both* of You.

Even my children don't wake me at 3 a.m. to share their anxieties or a painful rejection. They'd be welcome, but they respect my needs and know that they're more likely to command my full attention (and therefore get the best nurturing and advice I have to offer) if they wait until after breakfast. If you don't expect—or worse, demand—selfless giving from your spouse, you're more likely to get what you really need.

Every time my friend John calls, he asks me if I have the time to talk. If I say that I don't, he's never insulted, but asks when a more convenient time might be and calls back then. This trick of his has a miraculous effect: I never hide behind my answering machine when he's calling, because I know he doesn't expect constant availability and perfect attention. Since John doesn't expect heroic feats of attention, empathy, and perfect understanding from me at all times, it gives me great pleasure to give him what I can, when I can. I suspect that he extends a similar courtesy to his wife, which may be one of the reasons behind their long and successful marriage.

Don't Try to Compete with Distractions.

We know that men don't multitask as well as women do. Initiating a conversation while he's watching television, going over papers, or playing at his computer means that you're not going to be getting his full attention. This often doesn't occur to women, especially busy ones, in whom I have noticed exactly the opposite tendency. Some of the very best and most rewarding conversations I have had with my daughter have taken place while our hands were otherwise busy: cleaning up after a big holiday dinner, for instance. (It's one reason, perhaps, that quilting bees were such enjoyable social events for our female predecessors.) On the other hand, I've noticed that the communication—and the confidences—flow better in both directions with my son when there's no particular activity to distract us.

Sometimes distractions make it hard to have a certain kind of conversation at home or, in the case of a colleague, at work. If that's the case, remove yourselves entirely: Go for a walk or have a light meal or a drink somewhere else. A change of scene can really do the trick. My

British friends tell me that many of the substantive conversations in their marriages take place after dinner over a drink at the corner pub— or on the walk home.

Open with the Positive

A patient told me recently about a failed attempt she'd made to improve communication between her and her husband. She began the conversation by saying, "You have a history of not listening to me, so I've adopted some strategies in the hope of getting through to you." Needless to say, her overture was poorly received.

When we next spoke, I suggested that she try some version of the following: "There's a recurring issue in our relationship that I believe we can fix together, but I'd like to talk to you about the best way to handle it," before describing the problem. It worked. Her husband was happy to listen when his opinion was courted, instead of solicited after a criticism.

Ask for What You Want.

It's everyone's impulse—especially a man's—to want to solve a problem when they are presented with one. Unfortunately, a solution isn't always what you're looking for. Sometimes you simply want to vent some emotional steam or talk through a number of potential solutions to see which one makes the most sense. And sometimes you really are looking for help. *Tell your listener exactly what you want at the start of the conversation; it will help him to respond in the way you hope he will.* Say, "There are a number of different ways this could go, and I'd appreciate it if you'd listen to a few of the potential solutions I'm considering." If you really are stumped for a way out of a dilemma, ask him what he would do. In either case, you're likely to get the answer you need.

Say What You Mean

We know that men find it more difficult to decode nonverbal expressions than women do, especially those on the female face. Unfortunately, women tend to use a lot of these nonverbal signs to communicate. This can lead to a situation that both parties find very frustrating. You feel that your needs are being ignored, while he's exasperated by the subtlety of your cues.

So say what you're thinking—*out loud!* I have found that it helps a great deal to verbalize what I need, even when I feel the signals I'm sending are crystal clear. Saying, "I've had a really terrible day," works better than a hangdog look. And instead of casting a reproachful or injured glance after a man aims a painful barb my way, I try to *say* something, like: "That remark really hurt. Did you mean it?" Often, the response I get is a look of real surprise—more evidence that he wasn't ignoring my feelings but was just unaware of them.

I can't emphasize enough the importance of making it clear—*verbally*—when you'd like something or if something is bothering you. If he asks you what's wrong, and you say, "Nothing," chances are very good that he's going to believe you. That phrase is a conversation ender, like putting crime scene tape around what's bothering you. That doesn't mean that he doesn't care; in fact, it might mean the exact opposite. When men are upset, they tend to go it alone; the result is that they will respect your implicit instruction to leave *you* alone.

What message is it that we're really sending when we say that nothing's wrong, even when something clearly is? One possible interpretation stopped me short when I tried to shut my daughter out after an upsetting day seeing patients. "You're not really saying that nothing's wrong," she said. "You're just saying that *I* can't help you." She was right. Lost in my own emotional turmoil, I had unknowingly cast her as yet another irritant, something much more hurtful (and untrue) than I had intended. And even though she's not a doctor, talking about the intricacies of a particularly frustrating case that night did help me tremendously.

If you genuinely can't talk about something at that particular moment, say that too! "I've just received some very upsetting news, and I'm too devastated to talk about it right now, but I'll want your consolation and advice later. Can we talk about it at dinner?"

If you begin doing this, I believe that you'll notice a considerable difference in the quality of your communication with your partner, almost immediately—and a long-term benefit as well. There's a great deal of comfort and security in communicating with someone who's saying what they mean and not hiding anything up their sleeve. After a while, your partner will begin to trust that you say what you mean, and he'll relax, because he doesn't have to worry all the time that he's missing or misreading something.

Remember my friend John, the one who asks if I have time to talk when he calls? He also does me the tremendous service of *telling me* that he needs my urgent attention on those rare occasions when he does. I never have to hope I'm reading the tone of his voice correctly, because his verbal communication is reliable. It's yet another reason I'm always happy to hear his voice on the other end of the line.

Women tell me, "I don't want to have to ask him to unload the dishwasher. I want him to see that I'm tired, and offer!" Of course, it's lovely when the people in our lives anticipate our needs and go out of their way to do something special—even if it's a simple gesture, like making an unasked-for cup of tea. But expecting it without going to the trouble of making our needs known is nothing more than setting a trap.

Asking for what we need and hope for from a beloved partner is far more effective than what I call the global negative: "You never listen when I talk" or "You don't care about how I feel." As tempting as it might be to make an accusation like that, it only makes the accused feel that he can't succeed no matter how he tries. It'll be easier on both of you if you just ask him to put the dishes away.

Tailor Your Content

Men and women seem to be interested in different things, and this can manifest itself in conflict over the way we talk to one another. One of the first things we can do to address this difference is to make sure that we're tailoring our communication to fit our audience. You know exactly what I mean, because this is something we already do with our female friends.

Let me give you an example. I am perfectly capable of commenting on the cut of a new coat or the sophistication of a pattern on a silk scarf, but I don't share these details with my friend Anne, because I know that she's not at all interested in fashion. Correspondingly, Anne doesn't share her enthusiasm for the turbo-boosting options she adds to her computer except in the most general terms, out of respect for my lack of passion for the topic. We do talk—endlessly and to both of our tremendous satisfaction—about books. Anne and I are interested in different things, but we have found common ground.

Many relationships between men and women might also benefit from a similar sensitivity. Why don't we extend the same courtesy to our spouses as we do to our friends, by focusing our conversation on topics of interest to both of us? As I write this, there is a book of straight-talking relationship advice on the *New York Times* best seller list called *He's Just Not That Into You*. To borrow the phrase—and the spirit in which it is offered—I say to the woman trying to get her husband to keep up his end of the conversational bargain: "Maybe he's just not that interested in what you're saying!"

The same, of course, goes for men. One of my colleagues told me about a communication breakthrough he'd had with his wife. Between the staff at the hospital he works with and his patients, he comes in contact with thousands of people every day, while his wife is home with their children. "She was always asking me what was going on at the hospital, and then she'd be unsatisfied with my answers about our end-of-the-year projections and operating expenses. Over time, I realized that she wants me to tell her stories—about cranky patients, interesting case studies, staff gossip. So now as I go through my day, I mentally bookmark little things I think she'll like to hear later and bring them home to her. It's like bringing her flowers!"

By making sure he's telling her the kinds of things she likes to hear about, my colleague increases the amount of communication in his marriage and gives his wife some insight into the part of the day he spends away from her. His wife didn't want to audit the hospital's balance sheet; she was trying to get a fuller picture of her husband's interior life and emotions. So it probably isn't even the story of the cranky patient she enjoys, but hearing how he dealt with that patient and how that interaction made him feel.

One way, then, that we can improve communication between the sexes is to tailor the content of our conversations to our listener—just as I do with Anne.

Keep It Simple

Of course, there's a material difference between the way we talk to our female friends and the way we talk to our spouses; there has to be. I don't *have* to go shopping with Anne, but couples are mutually in-volved and invested in domestic matters, including parenting, pro-viding shelter for themselves and their offspring, and deciding how to spend money. We are, after all, in partnership with one another, so sometimes we have to bridge the gap by mastering a common lan-guage.

In most cases, men and women do understand each other, but I have found that when I make an effort to speak in a language men can easily understand, my message gets across more successfully. In my experi-ence, it's well worth the effort, just as it is worth it to learn any lan-guage. My school-perfect French may never sound truly "French" to a Parisian, but the practice I put into it makes it much easier for me to have a joyful time vacationing there than if I was reading phonetically from my guidebook. The visit is much richer for the time it takes to brush up on my vocabulary.

Let me use another example from the realm of female friendship. A female colleague of mine works at home. By now, I can basically tell by the tone of her "Hello" whether she's deep in the middle of a work project or simply unloading the dishwasher. If she's busy and there's a question I absolutely must ask her, I get right to the point. If she sounds like she has a little time to chat, I handle the conversation dif-ferently: I'll inquire about her family or our mutual acquaintances, mention a book or a performance that made me think of her, or share data on a mutual patient. I talk to most men the way I talk to my friend when she is busy. And here's what you can do.

• Make simple, declarative points, in order. If you want something done, outline it clearly and simply.

• Don't gild the lily, illustrate your points with anecdotes, or even use unnecessary adjectives. A poet I met once said he imagined that every word he wrote cost $20. I have found this a useful editing tool in my conversations with men.

Stick to the Matter at Hand

So many of the arguments we have with our male lovers and husbands stray from the topic at hand. Once you're angry, it's easy to get in touch with every single hurt feeling you've had in the relationship, and it takes a great deal of self-control to stop yourself from hurling old accusations, even when they have nothing to do with whatever sparked the original argument.

This can wreck real havoc on our relationships. I realize that banishing the memory—and the impact—of a previous argument or betrayal is easier said than done, but I suggest that you make an attempt, when you are arguing, to restrict your discussion to the immediate incident at hand.

Your husband may have made plans to play golf on Mother's Day last year, but that act of insensitivity has nothing to do with why he has once again forgotten to set aside time to pay the household bills. So the subject of that long-ago golf game should be considered off-limits for the purposes of your argument about the bills. If you can keep your request to asking him to plan ahead so that he can dispatch the domestic responsibilities he has assumed, your husband will really *hear* you on the subject, as opposed to tuning out, the way he does when you dredge up something he cannot change.

Believe What You Hear

I sat, mouth open in disbelief, as a friend of my daughter's described her first "relationship discussion" with the new man in her life. He had told her, point-blank, that the priorities in his life were his children from an earlier marriage and getting his new business off the ground.

The combination of the two meant that he didn't have a lot of time or energy for a serious relationship. In fact, the two most recent relationships he'd been in had collapsed because he hadn't been able to give his partners the time and attention they deserved.

I was dismayed to hear the way this intelligent young woman told her story and parried this man's every excuse with a reinterpretation of her own. She was intent on barreling headlong into a romance with him, despite the warning shot he'd fired across her bow at the very first opportunity. It wasn't a surprise to anyone but her when their liaison ended 5 months later, after countless broken dates and promises. He had told her everything she needed to know, right up front, but she had heard something else because she wanted to.

End the Conversation Before It's Over

Another source of discord between the sexes has to do with a difference of opinion about when a conversation should *end*. Because women are better at interpreting facial expressions and body language, you're going to know when he's becoming bored or losing patience with a conversation, possibly even before he does. You may just be getting warmed up, but when you notice the signs, it's best to wrap it up. Nobody's at their best when they're tired, and men seem to have less stamina for conversation than women do. If you'd like to talk more, ask him if he'd be amenable to continuing your discussion at another time. Sometimes it may take a few short conversations to get the job done—as opposed to the marathon session you might have had with a female friend—but you'll be pleased with the results.

Just. Stop. Talking.

Of all the arguments I have had with lovers over the years, one stands out for me. I made every single point I wanted to make, clearly and succinctly, and once I had made them, I turned around and went to sleep. It was astonishingly effective. I got everything I had wanted the next morning.

Unfortunately, I was never again able to replicate my success. What had gone so right that particular evening? I had undergone a minor medical procedure earlier in the day and taken a painkiller immediately prior to the argument. Ordinarily, an argument with this particular man made me very upset, and the topic under discussion was a particularly "hot" one. But in this case, the drug quieted the anxiety centers in my brain, which usually work in overdrive, so I was able to deliver my argument in a very cogent series of bullet points, as if I had been delivering a lecture from a set of PowerPoint slides.

I have taken the glorious memory of that argument with me into every argument I've had since, and now I give it to you. The lesson I took from it was this: Make your points as accurately and briefly as you can, and then stop. Stop talking, stop thinking, stop trying to get a response. Just stop.

Sum It Up

Given what we know about the differences between the way men and women remember, we can adopt certain tactics to make sure that we get what we need from one another, particularly in a disagreement.

For instance, after an argument, I find it very helpful to sum up my point of view with a closing statement, like this one: "I try to be kind to your family and there with you when they need us, because I know you love them. Please help me with mine. Not only would they appreciate it, but I'd be really happy for your help as well." Keep it positive and don't make your request or suggestion into yet another criticism. When you do that editorial work of boiling down many minutes of discussion into one or two succinct takeaways, you increase the chance that the conversation will stay fresh in everyone's memory.

Talk to a Friend

Loneliness is a disturbingly common thread in the conversations my patients have with me about the communication in their marriages. In fact, one of the most poignant things a patient ever said to me about her failing marriage was, "I'm lonelier when I'm with him than when I'm by myself." I hear echoes of this loneliness every time a woman says, "He doesn't seem interested" or "I always feel unsatisfied with the level of detail he's willing to get into with me." or "I just want to vent about my boss, but my boyfriend insists on telling me how I should solve the issues I'm talking about."

Wanting to share something with someone who isn't interested is, by definition, lonely. If the fashion-impaired Anne was my only friend, I would take her lack of interest in my new wardrobe very hard indeed. Thankfully, there are a number of people I can call who share my enthusiasm for the perfect cashmere sweater, so I don't need to bore Anne to tears.

Isn't that why you have more than one friend? Ellen might be a great wit, but she has no patience when you need help and advice; Alison is always happy to talk whenever you call for nurture and support, but she doesn't like to go out and do the things you like to do. Without being too Machiavellian about it, you need different things from different people at different times. If you have a variety of people in your life, then you can always acquisition what you need from the supply store. In fact, I have found that "using" my friends for what they can realistically offer protects them from the wear-and-tear that can happen when you demand things that they can't (or would prefer not to) give. If I want to attend a formal evening event, why should I drag a miserable Alison along with me, or chafe over a quiet dinner at her house, instead of asking someone who's likely to enjoy a glamorous evening out with me?

This seems logical, and yet I'm often surprised at people's extraordinarily high expectations for their romantic relationships. You don't expect everything from one friend, so isn't it too much to expect, except in very rare cases, for one person to satisfy all your needs—even when you have a special relationship with them?

As it turns out, there's a strong evolutionary basis for friendships, especially those between women. But biology aside, I believe that our friendships outside the relationship are some of the best psychological—and marital—aids on the market. And this is why I consider it such a tragedy when a woman lets her outside friendships languish when she gets serious about a man. It's not just those relationships that suffer, but also their romantic relationships and (perhaps most important) their own emotional stability and sense of balance.

If you feel lonely in an otherwise good marriage, consider finding a more receptive outlet for all your glorious talk. I urge my patients to join a professional association, a charity committee, or just to renew their acquaintance with old college friends. I tell them, "If your boyfriend isn't interested, find someone who is." One of my patients has done just that. She is an investment banker, one of the very few young women in her firm. Her weekly, girls-only poker game is the only thing that can get her out of her office before 9 p.m. She describes the camaraderie and support she finds at a table with other professional women as a "lifeline."

It's not the content of the conversation that matters so much—although I'd love to listen in when these women gripe about irascible bosses, recalcitrant clients, and independent-minded 3-year-olds. Mostly, it's the sense that they're not alone—and having the opportunity to talk in a way that they don't with the men in their lives. My patient has a lovely relationship with her husband, and they have lively conversations about many things. But she finds that 2 hours of five card stud with like-minded women scratches an itch for her that he cannot even find!

It's useful to remember that when you're looking for a friend, you don't have to find your soul mate, just someone who's going through some of the same things you are and whose company you enjoy. Many a young mother has found herself at a table at Starbucks with a woman she wouldn't have befriended a year before. The similar rhythms of their days and the comfort of conversation about breastfeeding or an article in the paper can make an otherwise improbable friendship possible—and increase the level of satisfaction they derive from the conversations with the men in their lives.

One last piece of advice? Be patient. These strategies work, no matter what phase of a relationship you're in, whether you're still in the first blush of romance or deciding to take your relationship to a more serious level, as we'll discuss in the next chapter. But whether it's your first serious discussion or the 4,000th, know that improving communication between the sexes is a process—one well worth undertaking, considering how rich the rewards.

5

Will You Marry Me?

Commitment (for Better or for Worse)

I have always loved men. I like the way they feel, taste, smell—and most of all, the way they think. Medical school was a vast garden of camaraderie and friendliness, where men of all sizes and shapes taught and mentored me and my (mostly male) fellow students. We were partners in a privileged fraternity, where intellectual achievement was the coin of the realm, and we built friendships laced with humor and a real, bubbling, intellectual excitement as we mastered complex information and solved problems with relentless logic. The men I studied and worked with made the whole process enormously fun and taught me a lesson I've carried with me ever since: Men can be wonderful friends.

But the minute I entered a personal, romantic, sexual relationship with any of them, all of that changed. As soon as the first flush of infatuation wore off, I felt isolated; what I thought was important for intimacy was never what my partner emphasized. Any sense I might have had of being comfortable, accepted, and understood mysteriously vanished. The easy exchanges I'd had with my friends were nowhere to be found in these increasingly unsatisfying relationships.

The problem seemed to get worse the more committed these relationships became! I began to believe that my friendships, so rich and replete with all the things that made my professional life so pleasant, were much more successful than my romances. I wasn't alone; many of my women friends, for all of their apparently successful attempts at partnering, confided that their relationships were not, in fact, all they seemed.

I am happy to report that I have gotten considerably better at negotiating my relationships with men since those years in medical school, and I have enjoyed many satisfying exchanges and relationships in the interim, but I find that I still struggle with those tensions. From the patients who pass through my office and the students I now teach, I know that it's not any different or easier for a younger generation.

Can we ever get what we want in a relationship from the lovers we adore? Or is there a reason that all the fairy tales end with a first kiss? Is a long-term commitment that continues to enrich our lives and satisfy our needs just a dream, or are there practical steps we can take to make sure that our increased familiarity with one another breeds not contempt, but intimacy?

Are We Working at Cross-Purposes?

If you believe, as I do, that the brain is sexed from the very moment of conception and that certain evolutionary processes have shaped the development of our brains and what they desire, then you might review the evolutionary and anecdotal evidence and arrive at a very uncomfortable conclusion: Women want relationships, while men do not.

On the face of it, there *is* a contradiction at work. From a purely evolutionary perspective, males are driven to mate as often and as widely as they possibly can, to maximize the number of their potential offspring. Females, on the other hand, benefit from pair-bonding, establishing long-standing relationships that will ensure them protection and resources, especially during the vulnerable period while they're raising their dependent young. On that evidence, it does seem that men and women are locked into a seemingly irresolvable conflict.

But I don't believe that all relationships are doomed from the start. First of all, this is a pretty reductive way to look at evolution. People, like animals, do all kinds of things that don't have anything to do with furthering the species. Witness, for example, the prevalence of homosexuality in the animal kingdom. June Reinisch, PhD, director of the Kinsey Institute for Research in Sex, Gender, and Reproduction in Bloomington, Indiana, offers this incomplete list: the fruit fly, some birds, bulls, cows, horses, antelopes, boars, rams, sheep, dogs, cats, and primates, including the stumptail macaque, pigtail macaque, rhesus monkeys, Catarrhine monkeys, Japanese macaques, Hanuman langurs, vervets, squirrel monkeys, chimpanzees, pygmy chimpanzees, and mountain gorillas. Bruce Bagemihl, PhD, has compiled a list of animals who not only engage in homosexual activity, but also live in pairs, defend territories they own together, and raise young together.

If homosexual behavior in animals is inherently counterproductive, why wouldn't evolution have extinguished it by now? I think this is a really important and unanswered question by critics of homosexuality, and it certainly highlights the flaws in a simplistic interpretation of the role human biology plays in the choices we make.

But let's say, for argument's sake, that it is true that women look for resources and security for her offspring from a man, and that this explains the drive so many women have to meet someone and get married. I think something very interesting is happening at this particular moment in time, right before our very eyes.

Since World War II, the economic situation for women has undergone a dramatic change (but not as drastic as it should, could, and will be). Our access to education and employment has exploded, with the result that a great many women now have the means to support themselves and their families. In this day and age, if a woman is dedicated to earning her own living, she is no longer dependent on a male provider. A variety of childcare options (again, not as many as can and should be available, but more than there have ever been) allow many women to go back to work not long after the birth of their children. (I'm a living example of this. I managed to give a lecture I thought was very important for my career while I was in labor with my first child—and to stay for the question period several hours later! I delivered the baby 10 hours after leaving the auditorium. A week later, I was back in my laboratory and seeing patients.) Maternity leave, once a fantasy, is now a reality and continues to improve as women fight for the right to have time they want with their newborns without losing ground in their careers.

Because women are much more economically independent than they have ever been, they are, as a result, much less dependent on a male partner. A woman's ability to support and provide for her offspring without a partner's help calls into question the *necessity* of marriage or a committed relationship for either sex. There is still a great deal of emotional and practical support to be gained from a pair-bond, to be sure, but there are a great number of single mothers who get by admirably by relying on their friends, neighbors, and family for the help a man might otherwise provide.

It's a terrific development, in my opinion, because it means that both parties can now enter into a long-term union out of *choice,* rather than obligation or need.

Consider, for example, one of my patients, Rachel. She is about to turn 40 and has not yet found a man she likes enough to marry and have children with. Since she owns her own residence and has job security as a teacher, she has begun to look into adopting. There are millions of children orphaned by the AIDS virus in Africa and by the tsunami in the Indian Ocean; if all goes well, she will be able to give one of those orphans a loving home before she turns 41.

I find Rachel's story fascinating, and indicative. Although she would like to have married by this time, she does not need a man for any of the things that her mother's generation believed you needed a man to have—a home, financial security, even a child. If and when she chooses to share her life with someone else, it will be because of what else he can bring, whether it's love, companionship, available sex, mutual interests, or simply a whiff of the unknown. And while I realize that many women have not yet achieved the kind of financial independence that she has, it's certainly the direction in which more and more women are headed.

For women currently in relationships, however, many of the problems remain the same. Is there anything in the current brain research that can help us to explain why the wonderful, heady passion of the first few years is so hard to sustain?

The Chemistry of Attachment

Lust is the spark that ignites between two people, and romantic love is the kindling. These drives begin the bonding process, and both presumably exist so that we can make babies and thereby continue to propagate the species. But once the wining and dining is over, and the seed for a new life planted, what is it that drives us to settle down?

One thing is for sure: That first flush of love—and the chemicals associated with it—don't last. Donatella Marazziti, a professor of psychiatry at the University of Pisa in Italy, and the researcher who discovered that men's and women's testosterone levels tend to converge when they fall in love, found 2 years later that although subjects were in the same relationships, their testosterone levels had returned to normal.

Thankfully, it doesn't have to be "game over" once those sexy hormones fade out. For some couples, of course, it is; about a third of all marriages fail in the first 4 years. That may be because a great many people are unable to navigate the transition into the next phase of love, which anthropologist Helen Fisher calls attachment.

This attachment phase, which also sees the abatement of the infatuation cocktail (dopamine, phenyethylamine, and norepinephrine), is accompanied by an increase in other chemicals, which work to strengthen the couple's bond, as well as the feelings of contentment and comfort that we have in the relationship. While these may not give us the speedlike rush of the infatuation chemicals, they are happy drugs in their own right. Foremost among the chemicals released during this phase are endorphins and oxytocin. Let's look at how they affect how we relate to one another.

Endorphins

I can usually get a laugh in lectures by reminding audiences that the endorphins that manifest after we've been in a relationship for a while are also known as "nature's painkillers." When we're in a relationship for a long time, the brain releases the same chemicals that enable a marathon runner to reach the finish line despite a stress fracture or a soldier to continue to fight even after being wounded. Draw your own conclusions!

Jokes aside, endorphins are pleasure-enhancing chemicals, and they have a powerful effect on our mood. We release them when we laugh, and when levels are high, we're social and friendly and relaxed. They're also released when we have an orgasm, and they share responsibility (with oxytocin) for the hazy euphoria we often experience after sex.

These natural painkillers also assuage the pain of social isolation, separation, and loneliness. Barry Keverne, FRS, has studied endorphins in female talapoin monkeys, who form close attachments or friendships with other females and spend hours a day grooming one another. When females are separated and reunited, their endorphin levels double. It feels good to be together.

Oxytocin

As you may recall from our discussion of sex, this hormone stimulates sexual desire in men and women, and the body releases even more of it during the sexual act and after an orgasm.

But oxytocin doesn't just show up when we're getting intimate; it also appears during a number of seemingly unrelated functions. For instance, it's associated with smooth muscle contraction during labor. Pitocin, the drug administered to induce labor, is an artificial form of oxytocin; the word *oxytocin* itself is derived from the Greek, meaning "rapid birth." Oxytocin stimulates the milk letdown reflex in a nursing mother, and it's released anytime we're under stress.

What's the connection among these disparate states? They're all times when bonding or establishing connections with other people might be useful, and oxytocin is the hormone that facilitates that bonding. For instance, researchers think that the connection between milk production and oxytocin promotes the mother-baby bond, and it may explain why nursing mothers have lower rates of postpartum depression than those who don't nurse.

Like endorphins, oxytocin feels great. If you're familiar with the wash of benevolence and love that you feel when looking at the sleeping face of your husband or baby, you know what I mean. Researchers actually refer to it as "the cuddle hormone."

One of the interesting things about oxytocin is how different the release response is in different people. Dr. Rebecca Taylor, a researcher at the University of California, San Francisco, did a small study in young women, asking them to remember two relationship events: one that had triggered positive feelings like love, and another that had triggered negative ones, such as abandonment. Participants were also given a 15-minute massage.

The oxytocin level results weren't that interesting: Negative thoughts did cause a drop, while positive ones had little or no effect, and the massage did increase oxytocin levels. What was interesting was *how widely the results varied among the participants.* Some women showed major fluctuations; others almost none at all. So the researchers set about trying to find out why.

It turned out that women who were unhappy in their relationships (reporting distress and anxiety) were also the ones whose oxytocin dropped when they remembered a negative thought. Women whose levels rose during the massage and when remembering positive memories were good at setting appropriate boundaries and at being alone, and they didn't try too hard to please others.

Does that mean that having access to this hormone encourages a sense of well-being in relationships? Or that being in a happy relationship encourages the production of oxytocin? The researchers did discover that women who were involved in a committed relationship at the time of the experiment saw their oxytocin levels go up more than the single women's did. From this they speculated that the intimacy of a regular relationship influences the availability of the hormone.

I wouldn't be surprised if further research uncovered that certain people have a genetic propensity to high levels of oxytocin. It would certainly provide us with a tidy answer for why some people find bonding easier than others do. Some—men and women—settle into long relationships like it's their natural state, while others chafe and struggle against the confines like a trapped animal. Perhaps there's a chemical explanation for these behaviors.

Researchers at the Karolinska Hospital in Sweden are working on oxytocin injections. They've found that a daily shot of the "cuddle hormone" lowers blood pressure and promotes relaxation in rats. While we're waiting for a human analog, it seems logical to me that a good way to elevate our mood in general and improve our relationships in particular might be to do what we can to keep levels of these feel-good chemicals high.

Here are some ways you can increase your hormone levels.

Exercise. Vigorous physical exercise is linked to an increase in endorphins. It's also linked to higher self-esteem and better sex— quite possibly as a result of all those endorphins. It's also a powerfully effective stress-buster, which is one of the things that gets in the way of us enjoying our relationships and having sex. As a doctor, I "prescribe" exercise to every single one of my patients, and I'm always gratified to see how the returns multiply for those people who take the advice.

Have lots of good sex. We know that oxytocin levels rise in both sexes during arousal and orgasm. I think of sex in a relationship as a feedback loop: You feel good about the person you're with, you want to have sex with them, you have sex, and you feel even better about them. There are added benefits as well, including a youthful appearance. A study done by neuropsychologist David Weeks at the Royal Edinborough Hospital found that couples who have sex at least three times a week look more than 10 years younger than couples who have sex less often.

A cuddle a day keeps the doctor away. One of my patients makes a point of getting regular professional massages when she's between lovers. She claims that it's a necessary expense, not an indulgence, and she may be right.

Kathleen Light, a psychiatry professor at the University of North Carolina School of Medicine, looked at oxytocin levels in women. Holding hands with their partners, maintaining eye contact, and lying together all raised levels, but the gold standard (an oxytocin production increase of 20 percent) was stroking of the hands, neck, or back—proof that touching doesn't have to be sexual to feel and be good for you. If you have a lover, encourage all these kinds of touching, then feel your blood pressure plummet as a result. If you don't have one, avail yourself of all the hugs and cuddles you can get from your kids or friends; it'll be good for all of you. Unfortunately, oxytocin seems to require someone else's touch, so there's no self-serve option here.

Bond with others. Your husband or lover isn't the only person who can increase levels of oxytocin and endorphins. Make sure that you have sufficient time for bonding with all the people in your life who are important to you, whether that's having a cup of tea with a beloved aunt, splashing around with your kids in the pool, or sharing a glass of wine and a long chat with a friend.

Some researchers believe that strong female friendships outside of marriage can actually help the marriage. Karen Roberto, PhD, director of the Center for Gerontology at Virginia Polytechnic Institute and State University in Blackburn, Virginia says that men cultivate friendships with other men until they're 30, but after that, tend to turn to the women in their lives—the wives, girlfriends, relatives, and friends—when they need emotional help and support. Women, on the other hand, continue to rely on female friends for support—sometimes *instead* of their spouses.

Going outside the marriage for friendship and support can lead to closer marriages, because it means that men don't have to shoulder as many of their partners' emotional needs. As someone once said, if you want to be happy for a day, have a good meal. If you want to be happy for a month, fall in love. If you want to be happy for a year, get married. If you want to be happy for a lifetime, make a friend.

Sex Differences and Oxytocin

Theoretically, if we do things that increase oxytocin production (like touching each other and having sex), we'll reap all the bonding benefits. But it never seems to work out quite that way in practice. Again, the differences seem to take place across gender lines. In fact, there is a significant difference in the way oxytocin works in both sexes, not because of the chemical itself, but because of the way it combines with the sex hormones already present in our systems.

Let's peek into a bedroom, where a couple has just finished having satisfying sex. With orgasm, their brains have released very similar floods of oxytocin into both of their bloodstreams. But once that oxytocin encounters the sex hormones there, the paths diverge dramatically, with opposite results.

The estrogen in the woman's blood magnifies and intensifies the effects of the oxytocin. Her blood pressure drops, she feels dreamy and relaxed, and she has an intense desire to continue bonding through cuddling, stroking, and talking. By contrast, the testosterone in the man's bloodstream (further elevated by the sexual activity, incidentally), neutralizes the oxytocin—and with it, the impulse to cuddle. In Dr. Light's study of oxytocin and blood pressure at University of North Carolina, men showed no increase in oxytocin production after stroking, probably because of the testosterone block.

So while the woman probably wants to curl up and further cement the bonding that's taken place, her lover feels no such urge and is already on the move, looking for the remote control and a snack. I think a lot of women experience this postcoital disinterest as surprising and hurtful, and I know a lot of couples have conflict about this. One woman told me that her husband's unwittingly dismissive behavior after a recent sexual episode was as shocking and cold as if he'd thrown a glass of water on her.

The effects of oxytocin are amplified by estrogen and counteracted by testosterone.

The answer, of course, is to meet each other halfway. Simply knowing that there are two different things happening to each of you is going to help alleviate whatever bad feelings usually accompany your postcoital ritual. Isn't his behavior automatically less hurtful when you know that the testosterone that makes him so sexy is neutralizing the chemical that makes you want to cuddle and whisper sweet nothings?

Whether that piece of information helps or not, you can both modify your behavior slightly so that you're both getting what you want and need. Tell him you want him to just "hang out" in bed for a little while afterward—say, 10 minutes—and then he can go do whatever he wants to. Or tell him to bring his snack back to bed. Alternatively, you can move to the couch with him and lay your head on his lap while you're watching television together.

Testosterone Falls

The release of endorphins and oxytocin aren't the only changes that come over us when we settle down into a relationship. Other hormone levels actually drop, and it's here again that we see the power of our experiences to modify our physiology. A team of anthropologists from Harvard University tested testosterone levels in a variety of men and found that married men had significantly lower levels than single men. When their marriages ended in divorce, levels rose again. As the researchers noted, this makes sense: Lowered levels of testosterone make it more likely that a man will spend time at home, as opposed to tomcatting around.

I was fascinated to learn that there was also a correlation between testosterone levels and the amount of time a man spent with his family. The men who spent the most time with their wives and children—the greatest "spousal investment," in the parlance of the study—had the lowest levels of all.

I wonder what effect this reduction in testosterone has on the couple. We know that testosterone is strongly related to sexual appetite; are these men reaching for their wives less often? We also know that testosterone is attractive to women, since women seem to choose men with facial types that indicate high testosterone. Are those wives finding their husbands less attractive as their masculinizing hormones drop? I'd be curious to know the answer. I know a great many long-standing couples with rich and intimate sex lives, so it might not be doing too much damage, but it is an interesting theory.

But, perhaps more important, the results of the Harvard study would seem to imply that *acting* like a good husband (by spending time with your family) makes it more likely that you'll *be* one. So act like you mean it! I find this to be a good rule in general. A friend of mine once told me about some advice she got from her rabbi, when she was questioning whether to make a charitable donation to a cause out of a sense of guilt. "You don't give to charity because you're a good person," he said. "Giving to charity—whatever your motivation—*makes* you a good person." I do believe that the more interconnected our lives are, the closer we become. I don't mean that we should live on top of one another, but it does make sense to me that a father who takes an active role in parenting and spends time doing it is going to have a closer relationship with his family—and have a better time doing it.

It's Not You—It's What I Need from You

A changing of the chemicals our brains release might explain why so many of my wonderful, challenging friendships and infatuations collapsed once they matured into full-blown, committed relationships. Here's some more food for thought: There's some evidence that what we want from our partner changes *as the relationship progresses.*

A study published in the *Journal of Personality and Social Psychology* sought to answer the question of how a secure marriage—one based on mutual knowledge, respect, and trust—could grow out of a courtship relationship, which is fundamentally based on putting your best foot forward in an effort to convince the other person to commit. It's a fascinating paradox, isn't it?

The researchers found that the self-reflection people wanted from their partners changed as the relationship moved from one phase to another. People who were still dating, in the courtship phase of a romance, were most intimate with partners who evaluated them favorably. They wanted someone who would tell them they were great. By contrast, married people in the attachment phase of the relationship were most intimate with partners who validated their own opinions of themselves. When they were dating, they wanted someone who would tell them they were great. They wanted someone who would agree with the way they saw themselves. When their own self-evaluation was negative, they were most intimate with a partner who agreed with that assessment.

This study provides one example of something I think is a very important insight: What we need from each other changes. Think about your relationship with your children, if you have them. The things a 2-year-old needs from you are entirely different than the things a 12-year-old is likely to need. Those needs aren't any less pressing, but they are radically different. Part of good parenting is making sure that you're meeting whatever needs your child is presenting *at that time.*

The same thing is true about a marriage. A long relationship isn't a static, dead thing. Like the brain itself, it's plastic and dynamic and changing all the time. As this study shows us, different behaviors are appropriate for different times. When you're dating someone, he wants to hear that he's the sexiest, strongest, smartest, funniest guy in the room, just as you want to hear that you're the cat's meow. But when you're married and there's more trust and dependency in that relationship, he's relying on you to tell him that he's got spinach in his teeth or that he perhaps needs to be more aggressive with his boss. So recognize that what you need from one another has shifted.

As you've probably gathered by now, I'm a big proponent of good manners in all relationships. Tact and diplomacy are very important to keep in mind when you're being "honest" with someone about their faults. First of all, wait to be asked for your opinion. If he doesn't ask for your thoughts, ask *him* if you can share some thoughts. If he says no (or says yes in a way that makes you suspect the real answer is no), respect his decision. If you do share your impressions of the situation he needs help with, please bear in mind that there's a difference between constructive criticism and being mean. You're in a unique position to help, but also to injure, so tread gently! And remember that no matter how intertwined your lives are, he's a separate person who makes independent decisions about his own life. Your opinions aren't law.

Your Cheating Heart

Sadly, no book on relationships can be considered complete without a few words about what happens when that commitment becomes too onerous to honor. It's sad but true: Love doesn't always work out, and even when we resort to the most heroic measures, we can't always save our relationships. Let's look at what goes wrong in relationships, why it makes sense to leave if you're unhappy and nothing is working, one way to decide to leave, and what grieving does to your brain.

Why Things Fall Apart: The Monogamy Conundrum

Infidelity, polygamy, cheating. Whatever you call it, it represents one of the most challenging aspects of marriage: the decision to have sex exclusively with one's marital partner. Failure to do so is the leading cause of divorce, not to mention the source of a tremendous amount of unhappiness within marriages that survive.

Psychologist Shirley Glass, PhD, has done a number of important studies on infidelity. According to her, the phenomenon is fairly common: Twenty-five percent of wives and 44 percent of husbands admit to having had extramarital intercourse. I suspect the numbers are much higher than that, and if I look at the relationships I've seen fall apart over the course of my lifetime, I'm pretty sure I'm right.

What's going on? Why are almost half of married men cheating? And why do women find it easier, or more advantageous, to stay faithful?

People (often those who are cheating, I've noticed) justify the high rates of infidelity by pointing to nature. "We're not meant to be monogamous," they say. "Life spans are twice as long now as they were at the turn of the century, and it's easier to stay faithful to one person for 20 years than it is to stay faithful for 40." They also cite the animal kingdom: "It's not natural to be monogamous; animals aren't."

Excuses aside, is there any evidence for—or against—humans preferring monogamy?

What We Can Learn from Animals

It is true that we often turn to the animal kingdom for information about why humans do what they do. We've done that many times in this book. But it can be irresponsible to extrapolate conclusions about human behavior from animals, and in many cases, it simply may not be relevant.

Animals don't compose symphonies or write novels or create public works, either—and many would argue that the formation of a family, whatever form it takes, is a cultural accomplishment of similar magnitude. Animals *do* sometimes have sex with their young, eat them, or leave them to die of exposure if they fail to thrive. Should we follow suit?

But to answer the "animals aren't monogamous" argument in the spirit in which it is offered, I would say this: Monogamy is "designed" to give the female protection during the vulnerable time while her offspring are raised. In many cases, a male animal does stick around for as long as that process takes. It's just that the offspring of animals grow to independence much more quickly than the offspring of humans do, sometimes in a matter of weeks.

Whatever its merits, this argument is losing its efficacy. As discussed earlier, women require less and less protection, and fewer resources from the men in their lives. One husband I know told his wife he had no intention of giving her child support: "That's going to be your punishment for leaving me," he said. Fortunately, she went on to earn about five times what he did and found that she enjoyed being able to give her children what she thought they should have without asking for help from anyone else. So perhaps the evolutionary need to have a man around while a woman's offspring are maturing is changing as well.

If I were cheating and looking for a convincing way to justify it, I'd blame my genes. Researcher Hans Hofmann, PhD, of Harvard found that there are two kinds of a species of fish in which a whole array of genes—as many as 100—collaborate to make some members of those species particularly attractive to the opposite sex. These extra-studly fish act just like the most popular boys at a suburban high school. They wear bright colors, bully their lesser-endowed peers, and aggressively court the female fish. At the aquatic equivalent of another cafeteria table, there's a different crew: the wimps. These have smaller gonads and spend the majority of their time swimming and feeding with other wimps.

This phenomenon isn't specific to fish. Among flies, there are "rovers" and "sitters." Sitters will become used to sugar and eventually will grow disinterested in it. Rovers, even if their proboscis is constantly stimulated by sugar, will continue to search for food; they never become indifferent to it. I'm not sure whether the science transfers, but the metaphor certainly does: People seem to be either "rovers" or "sitters." It's easy to sniff out an evolutionary reason for the rover: He's always at an advantage in a place where sweet things are scarce, because he's always interested and always looking, and that makes him very successful in locating and securing treasure. But you might not want to be married to one.

Is it any consolation to know that flirting behavior, fidelity, and jealousy may be at least as much a product of our genes as anything else? They used to say if you wanted to know what your wife would be like, you should look at her mother. Maybe you should look at the marriage of your potential spouse's parents to determine whether you're getting a rover or a sitter. And might there be a cure for an itinerant heart? Perhaps instead of couples therapy, the next generation will investigate the possibility of gene therapy for an errant spouse.

To be fair, it's not actually true that animals eschew monogamy. In fact, about 5 percent of all mammals *do* show monogamous, biparental behavior. One of them, in whom some of the most fascinating studies on the subject of monogamy have been done, is a creature called the prairie vole. (In case these animals and their ways begin to sound attractive to you, you should know that a vole is a rodent that looks much like a mouse.)

Prairie voles are largely monogamous. They form long-lasting pair bonds, even during nonfertile periods, and live in communal burrows. Once they've bonded, male prairie voles guard their female partners aggressively. They also participate actively in the raising of the vole pups, cuddling and grooming them alongside the females. Perhaps because of this, bonding between parents and pups is intense. Pups stay in the nest for a period of time after they've weaned and show extreme distress when separated from their parents. When a male prairie vole's partner dies, he will often stay single rather than mate again.

What makes the prairie vole the perfect husband? Neuroendocrinologist Sue Carter (and others) ascribes his behavior to a combination of hormones released into the bloodstream—different for males and females.

As you know, the hormone oxytocin promotes bonding, most notably between mother and child, but also between sexual partners. Humans release oxytocin in preparation for sex, and more during the sex act itself—and female prairie voles do too. They have quite a flood of this bonding hormone to contend with, because of the way they mate with their Mr. Right: often in marathon bouts lasting up to 2 days. There's a pretty clear connection between sex and bonding in the female prairie vole, and oxytocin is the reason why. When oxytocin is blocked, females won't bond, and when oxytocin is artificially administered, females will bond even without mating.

The brain of the male vole releases a hormone called vasopressin, which gets picked up in the areas of his brain associated with pleasure and reward. The release of this chemical becomes intertwined with the smell of the specific female prairie vole the male is mating with, so he feels that same sense of reward every time he smells her. (One of the men I once knew had a similar response to the perfume *Ma Griffe*.) That's what makes him faithful. She smells good to him and unlike anyone else.

Like oxytocin, the release of vasopressin is probably triggered during the sex act. Researchers know this because males change their behavior after they've mated. For instance, they'll act very aggressively toward other males after they've mated with their partners, while a virgin male will not. So vasopressin flips a switch that leads to a whole host of behaviors, one of which is monogamy.

The prairie vole is fascinating in its own right, but it's made even more interesting by comparison with a closely related species, the montane vole. These are genetically similar rodents with a slight difference in their brains—and vastly different mating patterns as a result. Male montane voles are irresponsible playboys: They're wildly promiscuous, antisocial, and play almost no role in the raising of their young.

What's the difference? Prairie voles have a lot of receptors for vasopressin, while the montane vole has much fewer receptors and doesn't have the same positive association with the female(s) with whom he mates, so he sleeps around. Administering vasopressin directly had no result: The key is in the way the brain is set up, not just in the plentitude of the chemical. The breakthrough was discovered when Larry Young, PhD, at Emory University put a prairie vole's vasopressin receptor gene and its regulatory region into montane voles. Once the voles had both the chemical and the receptors to "catch" it, Dr. Young saw a dramatic difference in their behavior. Suddenly, like their monogamous cousins, the montane voles became model family men.

So the next time someone cites the promiscuous animal kingdom to support their own straying, you can counter with the faithful prairie vole. I do find it of great interest that while the results are the same, the cocktail of chemicals it takes to make these rodents faithful is different for both sexes. I think of Wagner's opera *Tristan und Isolde*, and the drink that brought those two lovers together; I no longer believe that they had the same aperitif, no matter what Wagner says. Obviously, Isolde drank a draft of oxytocin but shrewdly gave vasopressin to Tristan.

The Future Is Bright

Given the differences between different types of voles, it's premature to draw any conclusions about human behavior based on these rodents. But we do know that oxytocin and vasopressin are major players when humans mate as well, and we have the same receptors as the prairie vole in our brains, even if they don't work exactly the same way.

It's certainly fun to speculate about what this research (and more like it) will bring for humans in the future. I could start a major business selling vasopressin receptor genes and its regulatory region to some of the couples I know. Perhaps the pharmaceutical companies will get wise, and "His and Hers" vasopressin and oxytocin receptor kits will be the *de rigueur* wedding present in 2050. Just to get the newlyweds started out on the right foot, you understand.

Not Just for Men

These are exciting days in the world of infidelity research. A sea of change appears to be taking place in who's cheating and with whom.

Cheating used to be a man's game, although researchers have long suspected that the numbers were higher in women than reported; men were just more likely to admit to an infidelity. Whatever the reason, the balance of those numbers are changing. Once again, the evidence shows that men and women are becoming more alike.

Additionally, the reasons *why* people cheat appear to be changing. Dr. Glass did a survey in 1980 and found that the majority of men who cheated were going after sex, pure and simple (she calls this nonrelational sex). These days, more men appear to want to relate, to form significant emotional attachments—even with their mistresses! The implications of this change may be reflected in the divorce rate, which is higher than it used to be. This isn't a man looking for a little sex on the side, but engaging in a serious relationship. These relationships are more time-consuming, more compelling, and harder to end—marriage material, in other words.

As women need men less for financial and social security, it's possible that men are motivated to hold on to the women they love with more ingenuity and persistence than they ever needed to before. It would be really fascinating to see if their brains were richer in vasopressin than those of their less-accommodating grandfathers—genes notwithstanding.

Is More Than One Partner Such a Bad Thing?

Here's a controversial opinion, based not on science but on my close observation of human relationships in 30 years of private medical practice: Sometimes monogamy isn't all it's cracked up to be. I know of a number of relationships where an "infidelity" actually supports and strengthens the primary relationship, instead of taking away from it.

In most cases, one partner has stepped outside the union for a sexual relationship that the other partner is no longer interested in having within the marriage. In some instances (more than you might expect), the other partner knows what's going on, but as long as "the cheater" is discreet and safe—in every sense—it's not a problem between them; indeed, they appear to be reasonably content with one another.

The extramarital relationship isn't always or exclusively sexual. For instance, I know a man who is tied, financially and emotionally, to a woman who is unwell. Because he feels he cannot leave her (and, in fact, doesn't want to), he has a close female companion with whom he does the things he cannot do with his wife. His companion, on the other hand, relishes living alone and has neither the desire nor time for a "full-time" relationship.

This option certainly isn't for everyone, but I think it is happening a great deal more than anyone thinks it is. It may present a solution for couples who can find solace and enjoyment in their primary relationship if their other needs are met in a secondary relationship. The danger, of course, is in keeping the balance, which isn't easy; the brain, as we saw, becomes addicted to a satisfactory lover, and sooner or later the demands for attention and more access to the beloved may shift for one of the players.

The true trick is to be content with what you have; I can't think of many relationships that are perfect in every respect.

Warning: A Bad Marriage May Be Bad for Your Health

When a relationship turns sour, it may be better to leave than to stay. The kind of marriage we're in matters, not just for our emotional health, but our physical health as well—especially for women.

Married people are healthier, overall. But just being married isn't necessarily enough: The *quality* of the marriage is important. A Canadian researcher found that people with high blood pressure in good marriages could lower their blood pressure by sharing an activity with their spouses. By contrast, the blood pressure of people in bad marriages rose when they were in their spouses' presence.

Women are particularly susceptible to problems in their relationships: Janet Kiecolt Glaser, PhD, has shown that newly married women with significant turmoil at home develop depressed immune systems and are ill more frequently than those in better relationships. A Swedish study published in the *Journal of the American Medical Association* found that female heart patients under marital stress were 300 percent—*three times*—more likely to have a heart attack than women in happier marriages.

Know When to Quit

The "one in every two marriages ends in divorce" statistic is held up as an example of how desperate the state of that union is in the United States. Frankly, I'm not sure. The research above would seem to suggest that staying in an unhappy marriage is bad for us, not simply psychically, but physically too. I think it's important for both parties to do what they can to make the relationship work, but I also think there's value in knowing when every avenue has been explored and it's time to part. As the song says, "Know when to walk away; know when to run."

One of my patients has spent the past 20 years in one of the worst marriages I've had the misfortune to witness. He is a lovely man and very intelligent, with a wide variety of interests—almost none of which he explores because he is trapped in this terrible relationship. His wife is very depressed (I'm guessing: She refuses to seek diagnosis, let alone treatment), and she is verbally abusive to him and to their children. Now, I'd never say anything unless he asked for my opinion, and I realize that I can't know everything that goes on between them, but I think he should take the kids and leave. Every day he stays with her inflicts further damage on himself and on the children.

Of course, there must be something about the relationship that satisfies him, or he would leave. (In that case, I would strongly urge him to do the work he needs to do to figure out what he's getting from this toxic relationship, and to find a less destructive way to obtain it from someone else.) But I suspect that his inertia has more to do with a fear of being alone—something to which women are susceptible even more than men (more on that to come).

A toxic relationship isn't the only reason to leave a marriage. Sometimes, as we get older, a basic incompatibility sets in. Different phases of our lives may very well call for different partners. If you're very lucky, the man you happily raised children with will also turn out to be an eager companion for trips to exotic lands during your retirement. But what if he isn't?

I know too many women who make unwise matches, simply because they're afraid of "spinsterhood," and too many women who stay in unhappy and unloving relationships, simply because they're afraid to be alone. I have spent some periods of my life in a pair-bond and some alone, and I can report with some authority that while it's not always easy to be a single woman in this culture, it can be very enjoyable a lot of the time. The key is to make sure that you don't go without the things that make life worth living: shared experiences and the society of others.

I make sure to see my children and my friends often, for long conversations and hugs. I have many male friends who provide me with an outlet for flirtation, even if there's no intent behind it. I know—and would like to remind you—that there are always opportunities for romance, love, and sex, no matter how long you've been "off the market." It's very important to me that I don't let being single hold me back from doing the things I want to do. For instance, I give lots of dinner parties, even when I don't have a partner to cohost, and I invite the most interesting people I know—including any eligible men I'd like to get to know better.

The happiest single women I know are those who have developed systems for navigating their way in a world that all too often seems set up for couples. For instance, I love eating in restaurants, but can find it uncomfortable when I'm alone, as many people do. I have put a little energy into establishing relationships with a few restaurants in my neighborhood, so that I'm comfortable there whether I'm with someone or alone. In fact, I'm quite sure that the service I get is better when I'm alone. The waiters know me so well that I sometimes wish for anonymity and fewer details about their personal lives! (A psychoanalyst I know has been going to the same restaurants around her office for the past 20 years. She sits alone, eats, reads the paper, and tips well. I'm always amused when I meet her for lunch, because a Diet Coke with a generous amount of ice and a wedge of lime invariably and magically appears before her as soon as we're seated.)

Deciding to Leave

Veronica, a friend and patient, is considering leaving her husband, who has a troubled relationship with money, but she is having a terrible time deciding whether a divorce is the right thing to do. I gave her Legato's Yellow Pad Exercise, which I will share with you now.

Take out a yellow pad and at the very top of the page, describe your problem as completely and clearly as you can. In Veronica's case, the principal problem is her husband Dan's financial irresponsibility.

On the left-hand side of the pad, make a list of all the positives the relationship holds for you. Veronica and Dan's sex life is great, and he always takes her side in disputes outside their marriage. He is a terrific, warm, and supportive father to their boys, and he is up at 6 a.m. on the weekends to coach their soccer teams.

On the right-hand side, list the cons. Dan lets bills pile up until they're so badly overdue that it jeopardizes the family's financial safety. Their phones and hot water have been shut off twice in the past year, and their mortgage company is threatening foreclosure—the precipitating event behind this particular crisis. The problem is not financial; Veronica thinks they have enough income to meet their expenses (despite the fact Dan routinely offers his services as a consultant for less than he should). Yet Dan is secretive about the family's financial status and has routinely refused to entertain the possibility of Veronica taking over these responsibilities. Another con for Veronica: Dan is a chain-smoker and pollutes the house with his habit.

Once the lists are finished, the next step is to look at the balance between them: Do the positives outweigh the negatives? What, if anything, in the list of negatives is so intolerable that you're not willing to endure it any longer?

Dan's chain-smoking harms not only his own health, but that of everyone exposed to his habit, but it wasn't a deal-breaker for Veronica. She was willing to negotiate some modification of his addiction that made it tolerable: not smoking in their bedroom, for example, but restricting it to the small study he kept for evening work at home.

The threat of losing her home, on the other hand, was unacceptable to her. This made all the positives pale into insignificance. Making that assessment was essential to addressing the problems that were destroying her marriage.

The next step in the yellow pad exercise is to outline *a solution* for the issues that are no longer tolerable. Veronica wanted to have a weekly meeting with her husband and a financial advisor about their financial situation until she was fully informed about every aspect of their resources and expenses. Once that was accomplished, she wanted to take over the full responsibility of managing the family budget.

But before she stages a confrontation with Dan, Veronica needs to have an action plan for a number of different outcomes. For instance, what will she do if Dan says no to her proposal? After a great deal of thought, Veronica has decided that if he refuses, she is prepared to walk away from the marriage. It's not an idle threat; she has really thought that decision through. She tells me that she and the kids can stay with her parents until they find a place of their own, and that her brother will lend her a little money to help them move and get set up. I told her that was too vague a plan and asked her to write out a very detailed description of how she will negotiate a separate life from Dan: her demands for a settlement, the lawyer she will use, how much money she will need short-term from her brother, and where she and the children (or Dan) will live once they've vacated their shared home.

This step—researching and constructing a detailed plan if negotiation doesn't work—is an essential part of the process. Often it leads people to decide they are not emotionally or financially equipped to actually separate from their spouses, and so they decide to live with the limitations of the relationships. This is a good thing to know before you deliver an ultimatum! But if you *do* feel the problems are intolerable, knowing precisely how you'll leave is very helpful to the negotiation. First of all, the spouse will sense a level of determination that might not otherwise have been there; and the spouse making the demands knows that he or she will survive if the significant other doesn't agree to the proposal or an acceptable modification of it.

The next step is for Veronica to schedule a conversation with her husband in which she clearly outlines her issues and tells him her minimal requirements for continuing the relationship. If he agrees to her stipulation, but doesn't keep the terms of their agreement, she should approach him again and let him know this is the last time she will do so. If the second attempt fails and her request to take over the family finances does not come to fruition, she has the security of knowing she has worked out a doable plan in which she can separate from Dan and—in spite of all the difficulties in doing that—survive on her own.

So what happened to Veronica and Dan? A real-life happy ending, which is to say that although they didn't ride off together into the sunset, Dan was able to comply with Veronica's requests, and their marriage is on considerably more solid footing than it was. This resolution didn't come without tension, but Veronica intelligently used every resource at her disposal. For instance, when Dan dragged his heels on presenting her with an accounting of their assets, she hired an accountant to "audit" them. In one Saturday, a professional was able to tell her exactly how much money they had and in what accounts, what was owed, and what was owed to them. He even gave them some tax tips! As Veronica had suspected, the problem was in the mess, not in a lack of funds. A bad chest x-ray gave Dan the incentive he needed to quit smoking (although freezing in the garage had probably made it less appealing). And they're going to a counselor together to try to figure out why they had to get so close to losing their marriage before they got together to make it work.

I'm happy to report that Dan and Veronica's marriage worked, but I was equally happy to have been able to give Veronica the tools to determine whether or not they should.

The Grieving Brain

The end of a romantic relationship is truly agonizing. I remember feeling furious as I imagined the cad who might one day break my daughter's heart. At the time, my husband consoled me by pointing out that she was 5 days old and safe—at least for a while.

Heartbreak really does feel like your heart is breaking, doesn't it? It's as if someone punched you in the stomach and, while you were down, told you you'd never amount to anything anyway. When you're in the thick of the grief that accompanies the end of a relationship, it's impossible to imagine that you'll ever put the pieces back together and go on with your life. It's not clear why it hurts so much, but one theory, by the great anthropologist Helen Fisher, is that ending a romantic relationship triggers the same feelings of abandonment and terror that we had whenever we were separated from our mothers at a very young age.

Researchers may have found another answer. It's difficult to study grief; as it turns out, time really does heal all wounds. That's good for the sufferer, but bad for researchers, who need to find study subjects in the throes of their sorrow. But the research that has been done shows that it's not just all in our heads. When we grieve, there is a real change

in what doctors call our "vegetative functions." Investigators studied
the brains of eight women whose relatives had died. The women were
asked to look at pictures of the dead people and pictures of a stranger
combined with words that were either related to the dead people or
"neutral." At least three different areas of the brain were involved in
the women's responses. Some were involved in processing the image
and coding it as a stranger or the dead person; other areas were needed
to interpret the words, while still other areas worked at recalling memories associated with the lost person.

Somewhat more surprising were signs that parts of the brain that
had to do with the regulation of the autonomic nervous system—
which controls things like our gastrointestinal activity, respiratory rate,
blood pressure, and heartbeat—had been activated. It seems that the
brain actually signals the rest of the body that something painful has
happened. This explains the physical responses we experience when we
grieve—a loss or increase in appetite, for instance. In some women,
menstrual periods stop.

As it turns out, the emotions caused by a terminated relationship
can actually trigger changes in the brain. Arif Najib, MD, a German
researcher, was looking for the connection between normal sadness and
depression. He asked women who were grieving about the end of a romantic relationship to look at a photograph of their ex and to think sad
thoughts about the relationship's end. He found that their brains
showed very similar activity—and that this activity was different from
the activity he saw when those same women were asked to look at a
photo of a friend they'd known for the same amount of time.

As expected, there was more activity in the areas of the brain that
control sadness. But there was also less activity in the amygdala, the
area of the brain that controls emotion and motivation. It's very similar to what happens in people who suffer from anxiety disorders, or

what we see when we look at the brain of someone suffering from post-traumatic stress disorder (PTSD). The more intense the grief the woman was experiencing, the less activity the researchers saw.

In general, it's a good idea not to make major decisions after any significant trauma—and I think we can safely say that the end of a relationship constitutes enough of a trauma to qualify. Dr. Najib's work suggests that parts of our brain shut down when we're grieving—hardly an ideal position from which to decide a major change.

So how can you best weather the loss, grief, and melancholy that follows the breakup of a pivotally important relationship—or, for that matter, any of the losses that attend even the happiest lives?

Try to get plenty of sleep. Even one night's disturbed sleep can elevate stress hormones.

Don't resume (or pick up) habits that can hurt you. For example, don't start smoking or excessive alcohol use. (When I asked one of my patients how she was coping with the terrible decision to institutionalize her mentally ill child, she told me she'd found that going to bed with a bottle of vodka helped. Needless to say, we had a long discussion about other, healthier options.) Don't use sleeping pills or other drugs for longer than your doctor recommends; if you are still having trouble after several weeks, find a professional with whom you can talk.

Avoid isolation. Even if your impulse is to distance yourself from other people. Talk to your friends. You may not be your usual, scintillating self, but this isn't the time to worry about being a burden. Get plenty of hugs, as well. Women whose husbands were undergoing treatment for cancer were found to have stronger immune responses if they had good social support.

Don't schedule elective surgery. Healing will take longer while you're under the stress of grieving even for a minor procedure like an eye lift.

Perhaps most important, postpone major life decisions. During the period immediately after a loss, the dopamine in our brains increases to help maintain our morale in the face of a disaster. This is helpful, but it can give us a false sense of clarity. That's why people cope through the wake and funeral so well, but collapse into sadness and mourning a week after the burial or the finalization of the divorce settlement. The pituitary gland then "turns on" the adrenal gland, the organ that is a factory for all the hormones we need to survive a threat. The stimulating hormones such as epinephrine increase, and so does cortisol, which can be particularly harmful if grief goes on too long. One of my patients sold her valuable home and the land on which it stood for a fraction of what it was worth just after the death of her husband. It was the wrong decision, emotionally and financially, and she regretted it bitterly.

A year after a loss, we should have recovered our balance. Even though the memory remains, and there are some sadnesses we can never really escape, the acute pain and disorganization that so disrupts our lives will fade with time. If it hasn't, or if things get worse, ask your doctor for help. It may be time for some real self-exploration with a professional and some medication that will break the melancholy.

The decision to end a long relationship—even when an ending is clearly the right decision—can be very difficult. I once thought, looking down at my 5-day-old daughter, that I would do anything to spare her the pain of a relationship's end. Now, with more wisdom (and having weathered more relationships—hers as well as my own), I realize that to do so would be robbing her of one of life's experiences—a bittersweet one, but a rich one nonetheless.

As you can probably tell, parenting my children has been one of the most fulfilling and enriching experiences of my own life. In the next chapter, we'll explore that wonderful adventure together.

6

Peek-A-Who?

The Changing Face of Parenthood

"How's that gorgeous baby?" I asked my patient Lucy. She beamed and said, "She's terrific. We're completely smitten with her, just head over heels in love."

I was struck by her choice of words. Poets often decry our use of the word *love* to define so many different states of emotion. How, they ask, can we use the very same term to describe both the passion we feel for a new lover and the fullness of emotion we feel when looking into the face of our sleeping child?

And yet, as Lucy knows, there can be great similarities between the two feelings at some times. Now new research shows us that what happens in our brain when we feel both kinds of love may actually be more alike than different.

You may remember the study by Bartels and Zeki that I cited in Chapter 2, where researchers asked participants who had recently fallen in love to look at photographs of their beloved so that the examiners could monitor their brain activity. The same researchers turned their inquiry to parental love in another, similar study. This time, they encouraged 22 mothers to look at photographs of their infants while their brain activity was monitored. They compared that brain activity with what they saw when the mothers looked at photos of other people: infants they had known for the same amount of time as their own, as well as their partners, best friends, and adult acquaintances.

What Bartels and Zeki found is that there are some very real similarities between what our brains do when we look at our lovers and what they do when we look at our kids. The orbitofrontal cortex, the part of the brain just above the eyes, is active when new mothers see their newborns—even just in pictures. This part of the brain, often known as "the emotional brain," also processes pleasant touch, pleasant smell, unpleasant smell, and facial attractiveness. (Disorders of this part of the brain may be involved in postpartum depression. Impairments to this emotional brain may blunt the normal bonding that goes on between mom and newborn.)

Perhaps most important, the same reward centers are triggered when we look at pictures of our babies and pictures of our beloveds. Love—whether it's for ruggedly handsome Mr. Right or a downy-cheeked 4-year old—feels really, really good. In fact, both kinds of love trigger the very same reward centers that light up when we taste a chocolate hazelnut bombe or get a massive bonus check at work—and help explain why a drug like cocaine is so difficult to kick.

There's another similarity between these two different kinds of love. If you remember, one part of the brain "turns off" when we're looking at a new lover: the social assessment mediator, which might otherwise cause us to note that his pants are too short and his chewing too loud. Our brains, in other words, don't allow us to make judgments that might threaten our love.

The same thing happens when we look at our child. This certainly explains that particular brand of parental blindness that makes our wrinkled, red newborn the most beautiful one on the ward, our toddler the most precocious, and our teenager the most attractive and interesting. (Some people have this affliction worse than others do: I finally met one couple's daughter after hearing over-the-top descriptions of her extraordinary beauty, wit, charisma, and charm for years and discovered a perfectly nice, but very ordinary kid. Somebody—I plead cowardice—should tell her parents.)

There are some very real differences, thank God, between the way we feel when we hug our child and when we fall into bed with a lover. Most important of those is that the part of the brain that controls the hormones associated with arousal, like testosterone, isn't activated.

Do Women Care More?

One of the biggest questions I'm asked by new mothers is, "Why does it seem that I feel more strongly about the baby than my husband does?"

I often hear from women, astounded by what they perceive to be a lack of feeling on their husbands' part. "Leaving her is the hardest part of my day, but he blows right out the door without looking back. If I hadn't called him back this morning, he wouldn't even have kissed her good-bye," one patient told me in tears. In the argument that began this book, the simple question of washing a small child's hands turned into a much bigger debate about potential health hazards and learning self-care—for the child's mother. Her dad just saw a kid eating with dirty hands.

My patient Allie related another striking example—perhaps more striking for its everydayness. She and her husband alternate who gets up early with their 2-year-old. Allie always runs into her daughter's room as soon as she hears her cry; she can't bear the thought of their daughter waking up and thinking she's alone. Her husband, on the other hand, takes his time getting out of bed, brushes his teeth, and puts on socks and a robe before going in to get her. Listening to their daughter call in vain on the baby monitor while her husband does his ablutions drives Allie insane, but their daughter has caught on: She begins by calling for Mommy, but if nobody comes right away, she knows it must be Daddy's morning and switches to calling him instead. Children are nothing if not adaptive, and I think it's a good example of how we can learn from one another's parenting styles; it's not a bad thing for Allie to realize that the baby won't burst into flames if she finishes what she's doing before running to her side.

It does seem to be true that men parent *differently* than women do. They talk less to their children and roughhouse with them more. They tend to give their children more independence than their mothers do, even when the child is frustrated. These differences, of course, create a feedback loop. In a study done at Boston Children's Hospital, infants relaxed when they were approached by their mothers (their pulse and breathing rates slowed down, and their eyelids lowered). By contrast, when their fathers came into the picture, they began breathing more quickly, they tensed their shoulders, and their eyes widened, as if they knew something exciting was about to happen!

Certainly, much of the difference in how we parent has to do with our socialization, from early infancy on—in other words, how we were parented. Girls are given dolls and stuffed animals as toys, while their brothers play with trucks. Parents are more nurturing with girl children, which in turn teaches them how to be nurturing—first to their

Nature versus Nurture?

Perhaps no question sparks more controversy than whether children assume sex roles as a result of their biology or the socialization they're exposed to. The answer, of course, is probably not an "either/or" but a "with"—some combination of the socialization we receive interacts with our natural biology (itself a knot of complicated and intertwining factors) to turn us into the people we become.

Parents are quick to call "nature," possibly because we don't want to acknowledge that we treat our boys and girls differently. It seems that every one of us has a story about toys and young children like the one my favorite pediatrician, Dr. George Lazarus, shared with me. A very modern and enlightened parental pair presented their young daughter with a set of wonderful toy trucks. Several hours after she had unwrapped the present, the parents noted that neither the toddler nor the trucks were anywhere to be found, and the child's room was darkened and silent. The little girl met them at her door, pointing to the four trucks under the covers in her bed: "Shh!" she cautioned her parents. "They're sleeping." Another mother told me, laughing, of finding her 21-month-old daughter's shiny new Tonka front loader wearing a frilly white diaper cover taken from the laundry hamper.

As much as some dispute the existence of the "feminine" and "masculine" brain, we're at a loss to explain how many of these same biases show up in the animal kingdom, if there's no biological imperative. UCLA psychologists Gerianne Alexander, PhD, and Melissa Hines, PhD, did an experiment in which they presented vervet monkeys with six toys. The males played more with the truck and ball, while the females chose the doll and a pot; gender-neutral toys (a book and a stuffed dog) got equal attention. Certainly, socialization didn't influence these subjects!

We see the interaction of socialization and biology in the following research on rats. Mother rats lick the anogenital area of male pups more than they do those of their daughters. They can detect the smell of the breakdown products of testosterone in the urine of their newborns. It seems that this licking helps neurons survive in an area of the nervous system (the SNB system), which enervates the penis. This nerve cluster is, for obvious reasons, larger in males. If the mother rat cannot smell, she won't lick her pups as much and can't favor her sons with more licks than she does her daughters. Her pups will grow up, whether male or female, with smaller, female-like SNB systems. In other words, the way the rats are treated (licked or not) directly influences the biology of their sex.

If it is true that human parents treat babies differently from the day they are born depending on the child's sex, then the lesson we can take from these rats is that all the ways in which we stimulate and interact with our children may have an impact on their gender-specific differentiation and behavior. ⤸

teddy bears and younger siblings, and later to children of their own. Little girls are encouraged to empathize, and signs of aggression are suppressed by parents and teachers much more actively than they are in their little boy counterparts. So by the time we're grown, our roles are clearly defined for us, and even the most conscious and enlightened of us find ourselves transmitting many of the same gender-specific messages to our children. If you're parenting a young child, these are biases to watch out for.

But there may be a biological component to these differences as well. One of my patients, a supremely intellectual academic, took enormous pleasure in her new motherhood, because she said it made her feel "feral"—animalistic and instinctive for the first time since her own childhood.

Mothers do have a very deep synergistic and symbiotic bond with their babies. Mark George, MD, did a fascinating experiment using brain scans of new mothers, who were exposed to the sound of their babies crying. These results were then measured against the reaction in the brain when the mothers were played another audio tape—this time, the sound of babies crying, but scrambled so as to be unidentifiable. The same areas lit up; the women's brains could decode the signal, even when the ears could not.

What Roles Do Hormones Play?

One of the very basic differences between men and women lies in the hormones we release at various times. These differences are exaggerated at certain times in our lives—including during pregnancy and in the few months after birth. The difference in these hormone levels may provide us with further explanation for the difference in parenting behavior—and, as you'll see, for some surprising similarities between us.

Remember our old friend oxytocin, the bonding hormone? This hormone, released when we are sexually aroused and when we make love, is also a powerful driver in the series of caretaking activities that make up parenting behavior—especially caretaking behaviors in the mother. The activities associated with having a child—pregnancy, birth, and breastfeeding—cause oxytocin levels to skyrocket in women. And when those levels go up, the brain is ready for it: During pregnancy, women produce more estrogen than usual. Researchers believe that this increase in estrogen prepares the brain to receive increased oxytocin, by upping the number of oxytocin receptors in the brain.

The influence that oxytocin has on our behavior is arresting. Let's look (as I do whenever I want to feel warm and fuzzy) at rats. There's a fairly stark difference between a mother rat and a virgin, or nonmaternal, rat. The mother rat will take care of any babies placed into her nest, even if they're not her own, and will choose her pups over food. She is an aggressive defender of her young and will attack anything she perceives as an intrusion on her nest. A nonmaternal rat will not only choose the food every time, but will withdraw from youngsters, in the best-case scenario, and eat them, in the worst. (I remember watching a childless female friend hold my newborn son as if he were an extremely volatile collection of high-impact explosives. It didn't occur to me to be grateful that she wasn't hungry!)

Oxytocin drives these maternal behaviors. When the natural production of it is blocked (in sheep and in rats), mothers reject their own young. When oxytocin is injected into nonmaternal rats, they will begin to treat pups as if they were their own.

Oxytocin has a similar effect on humans. As a woman breastfeeds, oxytocin levels rise in her blood, stimulated by her infant's sucking. The oxytocin directs the milk glands to release milk and has a profound effect on her behavior as well. According to a study done by Kerstin Uvnas-Moberg, MD, PhD, at Karolinska Institute in Sweden, a nursing mother will score higher on a psychological test designed to measure her urge to please other people. The higher the level of oxytocin in her blood, the lower her blood pressure and the more relaxed she is.

Testosterone, if you remember, blocks the effects of oxytocin—the reason that your husband's impulse is to order a pizza after sex (or perhaps worse, fall asleep), while you're still in snuggle mode. Testosterone's blocking effect may also be why women seem to bond so much more intensely with their newborns than men seem to.

Another chemical associated with pleasure increases in a specific part of the brain when rats groom their babies. We've discussed the neurotransmitter dopamine before; it's highly associated with motivation, pleasure, and reward (and often addiction). Dopamine increases before the rats begin the grooming session, and the amount of dopamine they release corresponds directly with how long the grooming goes on. For the human equivalent, watch a new mother gently stroking the back of her new baby's hands while she admires his perfect, miniscule fingers.

I wonder if the number of dopamine and oxytocin receptors that individuals have in their brains is the neurological basis for differences in maternal behavior. It's certainly true that not every woman experiences motherhood in the same way. I remember running into a friend of mine from college with her three children, all under 5, and realizing that she looked better than I had ever seen her—a beatific Madonna with green pea puree on her sweater and jam in her hair. She had taken to motherhood like a duck to water and confessed to me that she'd never been happier.

But I know other women who have a much more difficult transition. They miss the privacy and freedom of their pre-baby lives and find the day-to-day care of a young child boring, depressing, or frustrating. There are certainly social factors that contribute to the disparity. It's much harder to enjoy motherhood when money is tight and emotional resources are spread thin. But many of the women I know with this uneasy relationship to motherhood aren't coping with those issues; they simply don't enjoy it as much. I wouldn't be surprised to discover that perhaps women who enjoy motherhood less have comparatively fewer receptors for these pleasurable bonding hormones than the beatific Madonna-types do.

Certainly, most of us fall somewhere in between. There's no question that motherhood is one of the most satisfying, enriching, gorgeous gifts we are lucky enough to receive in this lifetime, but it also requires tremendous patience and some very great sacrifices. (And some small ones. A new mother in my practice wailed that she just wanted one simple thing: to be able to close the door to the bathroom while she was using it.)

I was fascinated by the results of a study published in the journal *Science,* in which 900 working women reported what made them happy over the course of their days. Not surprisingly, housework and commuting ranked low. Perhaps more surprisingly, watching television alone ranked very high, above shopping and talking on the phone. One of the most surprising findings of all came from the parenting realm: For these women, taking care of children ranked below cooking and just above housework—very low on the overall scale. Income and job security didn't seem to make a difference, but other factors did: sleeplessness and tight work deadlines significantly reduced the amount of pleasure that women took in pleasurable activities, like watching television.

It shouldn't detract from the wonderfulness of parenting to say that it's a lot of hard work. I think it's absolutely essential for parents—especially new ones—to get the support they need. After all, we're not supposed to parent alone. Many European countries encourage fathers to stay home for months after the baby is born. In many other cultures, it's traditional for multiple generations of families to live together, so that there's always an experienced aunt or older sister or mother or grandmother to help with housework and infant care. In fact, the tricky late afternoon hours when newborns are likely to fuss for no reason is still known colloquially as "grandmother's hour." Ideally, a tired new mother has her own mother (or someone else) around to make her a cup of tea and to take a turn walking and soothing the baby.

Unfortunately, the American emphasis on the nuclear family, and the likelihood that young parents are raising their children some distance from their own parents, means that women are often robbed of a very valuable resource. We see this most dramatically in studies of women with postpartum depression. Societies in which strong female support networks are reinforced have reduced incidence of this type of depression; in our society, women who feel socially isolated are more at risk of developing it.

New mothers, if nobody else has told you this yet, I will: New mothers, it's *okay* to feel resentful, tired, and bored by the responsibilities of parenthood sometimes. It's natural to feel angry when a delicious and healthful homemade meal is flung on the floor or a soccer jersey goes astray—again. Having these feelings (and voicing them) doesn't make you a bad mother!

In fact, getting some of the pressures off your chest can significantly improve the time you spend with your child. Find someone with whom you can talk about the difficulties of this very challenging job—whether it's a sympathetic friend, another mother, or even just your personal journal. There has been a proliferation of blogs devoted to just this topic, and I think it has something to do with the relative anonymity of the Internet, combined with the feeling of community. It feels really good to admit that you're going to scream if you have to listen to "Elmo's Song" one more time, and it feels even better to get hundreds of supportive and understanding e-mails from women who are listening with gritted teeth for the 200th time as well.

It's very important for women to get the support they need—not just for their own mental health, but also because maternal behavior does have a strong effect on a child. Depressed mothers smile less frequently and interact less often with their infants. Children of depressed mothers have lower IQs, watch more television, and are more likely themselves to be depressed in adolescence.

Mother mice lick and groom their babies; if they neglect this little piece of parenting, the babies grow up to be terribly anxious. Why? Because the genes that make receptors for the "stress protein," cortisol, which soothes us, is deactivated soon after birth. Without proper care, the receptors are fewer in number and quite possibly not as effective in latching onto cortisol as the normal receptor. When stressed in adult life, these mice become very anxious! Sadly, we know from children who have been neglected, without the usual profusion of parental kisses and cuddles, that there's a human correlation as well.

Anything Mommies Can Do, Dads Can Do Too

Oxytocin does play a major role in mother-child bonding, but it certainly doesn't mean that men can't parent as well as women can. In fact, there's very real evidence to the contrary.

At least part of this has to do with changing circumstances. I believe that men are better parents now because they have the opportunity to be better parents. No longer the absent breadwinners of the hunter-gatherer era (or the 1950s), they're taking a much more active and participatory role in childcare and child-rearing. I have a number of male patients who work from home and end up handling the lion's share of the domestic and childcare responsibilities because it's easier, more convenient, and more efficient for them to do so. One of the men I treat has put his career on hold so he can stay home full-time with his two young children; his wife makes enough to support them both.

Additionally, many of the provinces traditionally reserved for women are now shared—with the result that men can share in the bond that was traditionally reserved for the mother. For instance, the feeding of a young infant is an ideal time to bond. It's a natural time-out, tailor-made for face-stroking, whispering sweet nothings, and making lots of intimate eye contact. For centuries, this was the exclusive province of women; now, it's just as likely to be Dad at that 3 a.m. feeding, cooing nonsense and holding the bottle.

One of the long-standing arguments that evolutionary psychologists have given in defense of traditional gender roles (which assume that the woman will take responsibility for childcare) is that women take greater parental investment because their maternity is guaranteed. A man may have a shadow of doubt in his mind about his paternity (at least until he sees his Aunt Tillie's chin on his daughter's tiny face), but there's never any question at all who her true mother is. Of course, the ready availability of accurate DNA testing makes even this far-fetched argument obsolete.

Some new research even suggests that the hormonal changes that accompany pregnancy and birth in order to prepare a woman for motherhood may not be happening just to women. For instance, Canadian research suggests that men go through some of the same hormonal changes that women do in anticipation of, and in reaction to, a new baby. Psychologist Anne Storey tested the hormone levels of more than 30 couples over the course of pregnancy and after birth. The hormones they concentrated on were cortisol, prolactin, and testosterone. Here's what they discovered.

• **Cortisol:** The "stress hormone" plays a noteworthy role in the parenting process. Alison Fleming interviewed first-time mothers to see how they felt about and interacted with their babies, and she discovered that the most responsive and sympathetic mothers were the ones with the highest levels of cortisol. This makes sense: Although we think of stress as a bad thing, it's really just a signal our body gives us to pay attention and may help a new mother to be alert and attentive to her infant. (My super-intellectual patient told me she felt positively wolflike in the days after her child was born. She said she felt she could scent danger in the air and that her reflexes had never been as acute. This may have had to do with her elevated cortisol levels.)

Elevated levels of cortisol at this time make further sense, given what we know about this hormone's ability to promote memory. It may speed the rate at which we learn the basic baby husbandry that seems so overwhelming at the beginning of our children's lives, and it may guarantee that we retain it long after our own mothers or baby-nurses have gone home.

• **Prolactin:** Prolactin (as the name would suggest) is a crucial component in nursing and lactation. It also contributes to nurturing and caretaking behaviors. For instance, researchers have found elevated proactin levels in birds that take care of eggs and nestlings, even when they're just the babysitters, not the parents. The parents had the most prolactin, but the most helpful caregivers were second; the least helpful had the lowest levels. What researchers don't know is whether high prolactin levels make for good caregivers, or if there's something about all those hungry baby bird mouths that provokes the release of these hormones. They suspect it's a combination of the two.

• **Testosterone:** Testosterone, of course, is linked to aggressive, dominant behavior and exaggerated territorial defense; the more testosterone a man has, the more apparent these behaviors are. In certain contexts, aggression and violence might be good attributes for a parent to have, but high levels might not be ideal in the first few days and weeks of a new baby's life.

The results of Storey's study are fascinating. In women, cortisol and prolactin levels naturally increase during pregnancy; according to the study, men's do too! The men's prolactin levels rose approximately 20 percent in the 3 weeks before their partners gave birth. In the same period, cortisol was also twice as high as normal in the expectant fathers. During the 3 weeks after birth, testosterone levels decreased significantly—33 percent—in the men. (Levels returned to normal in the next few weeks.) Sociologists at Harvard University have also found that single men have higher testosterone levels than married ones and that fathers have the lowest levels at all.

In another study, done by Storey's colleague Katherine Wynne-Edwards, PhD, fathers were found to have higher levels of estrogen than other men, beginning about a month before birth and for up to three months afterward, mirroring a similar escalation of estrogen in their pregnant partners.

These hormone levels do affect parental—specifically, paternal—behavior. Storey asked men to hold dolls wrapped in recently worn baby blankets (or their actual newborns, if they were born), listen to a tape of a crying baby, and watch a tape of a newborn trying to nurse. The men who said they most wanted to comfort the crying baby had the highest prolactin levels and the biggest drop in testosterone.

I will admit that I was slightly incredulous when Alex, one of my male patients, came in complaining of weight gain, swollen ankles, and early morning nausea after his wife became pregnant. But there is a fairly well-substantiated history of these sympathetic pregnancy symptoms. A study published in the *Annals of Internal Medicine* reported that more than 20 percent of men had experienced some symptoms, like morning sickness and weight gain. These real-life symptoms may be explained by the real-life change in men's hormonal levels.

What causes this change? Researchers believe that hormone changes are triggered by the changing hormone levels in a man's partner and that the signals may be communicated through pheromones. In other words, the approaching birth sends signals that prepare a woman for motherhood; she, in turn, prepares her partner.

There are clear evolutionary advantages to this. In more primitive societies, babies whose fathers stuck around in the weeks after birth were more likely to survive. According to the research, there's still a convincing argument for paternal involvement; children with involved fathers do better in school and socially (although I certainly know a great number of children raised without them who excel in both academics and their social relationships).

Ross Parke, PhD, has done a great deal of research on the way men and women parent, and he has consistently found that men are equally capable of interpreting and responding to the needs of a new baby. This is supported by Dr. Fleming's experiments, which measured the hormone levels and emotional responses of men to the sound of a baby crying. Men who had children responded more dramatically than men without them, and experienced fathers responded much more dramatically—both emotionally and hormonally—than new dads. Their prolactin levels rose, and they felt a greater need to comfort the crying baby. Whether experience has changed their biology or prolonged exposure to babies has made them more sensitive to the signals is unclear. But Dr. Fleming feels that involved parenting is sort of a self-fulfilling prophecy: The more you do it, the better you get at it, and the more you enjoy it, which makes it even more likely that you'll want to do it.

Perhaps most important, the baby doesn't differentiate in any important way between mom and dad. In a Newborn Intensive Care Unit with insufficient incubators, premature infants were wrapped up, skin to skin, with one of their parents. The results were surprising. Far from suffering from the lack of equipment, the cuddled babies thrived, and now a few hours a day of "kangaroo care" has become a gold standard for preemie care. Both mothers and fathers are encouraged to participate. Babies gain just as much weight if they're cuddled up with their fathers as their mothers.

So if the dad in your family is ready and willing to participate, *let him*. It will make all of you happier!

A Letter to Parents:

I see my patient Monica fairly often; she has a chronic condition that needs close attention. Since she showed some interest in the factoids I was uncovering while researching this book, it became habit for me to share a new tidbit with her when she came in. A few months in, she sheepishly confessed that all this new information was helping her with a relationship in her life, not with her husband, as you might expect, but with her teenage son. For instance, she claims that learning to "sum up her argument," as I suggest women do when they're concluding a fight with a man to compensate for men's less-than-perfect memories (and our very good ones), has made a night and day improvement in their relationship. Her son is finally really hearing her, with the result that she doesn't constantly feel that she has to nag him about the issues under discussion.

I wasn't surprised to hear that this information helped Monica's relationship with her son. Parenting a child of the opposite sex can be fraught with many of the same difficulties that plague our romantic relationships. Some of the information in this book can help you to understand why your son does what he does—and why you respond the way you do. So don't hesitate to use whatever advice seems likely to improve the communication in those very important relationships.

My patients often ask me how to parent in a "gender-neutral" way, and I tell them the truth: It's a) not really possible and b) probably not desirable. That said, there certainly are things that we can do to make sure that our children of both sexes enjoy opportunities as equal as we can make them. I think there's altogether too much pressure put on parents (particularly mothers) in this culture as is, and I don't mean to add to the pile, but I do think that maintaining an awareness of cultural stereotypes, and making a conscious effort to counteract them, is work well worth doing.

Countless studies have shown us that parents treat children of different sexes differently, and anyone who has parented both (as I have) knows that you can find yourself treating boys and girls differently, even without realizing it. A woman I know did what I think is a very interesting, if unscientific, experiment. One Saturday, she tried to pay attention to everything she said to and did with her daughter, asking herself the whole while, "Would I have suggested this activity if she was a boy? Would I have said that to her if she was a boy?" To her surprise, she found that she did encounter a number of situations—in the pictures she chose to point out in a favorite book, for example, and in defusing a playground conflict—that she thought she might have han-

When Two Boxes Aren't Enough

I recently gave a lecture in a small Midwestern city on the subject of how the brain becomes male or female. A woman came up afterward to talk to me, saying that she was tremendously concerned about her 6-year-old daughter, who was persistently and insistently asking if she could become a boy. The child had even inquired about operations to achieve this end, saying that she was really a boy in her head, and not a girl at all.

In our conversation, the mother showed no trace of displeasure or embarrassment about her little girl's predicament, only love and empathy. She asked me if some fundamentally important event had happened in her daughter's development to make her sense of her own gender discordant with the body she was born with, and whether her little girl might, in fact, be more comfortable as a boy. Where, she asked, could she get expert advice about how to help her daughter?

These aren't easy questions to answer. I do suspect that something happened over the course of the sexing of her daughter's brain to create the discordance. As to whether she'd be more comfortable as a boy, only time will tell; many transgendered people who apply for sex reassignment surgery knew from the time they were very young that their bodies didn't match their sense of themselves as male or female. I advised her to start her search with a knowledgeable and sensitive pediatrician.

I left the lecture hall feeling tremendous respect for that parent. She had spoken of her daughter with such compassion and had such an interest in her child's comfort that I felt she would get her daughter the appropriate help. My only concern is that our own understanding of the brain is still so limited—in spite of the tremendous advances neurobiologists have made over the past few years—that we may not yet be able to help as effectively as I would wish.

I am interested in what makes us male and female, and yet I am constantly reminded that those might not be the only boxes. Sex is, after all, a continuum—

dled differently, if her daughter had been her son. If she parented more consciously afterward, the experiment was a success.

I think that the best we can do as parents in general, and certainly in this particular area, is to provide our children with as wide a range of opportunities as we can, right from the beginnings of their lives.

and gender, even more so. After another lecture on what sexes the brain, I engaged in a very stimulating debate about what makes someone "male" or "female" with a man who told me that he had been born with ambiguous genitalia. The medical term is "intersex," which designates individuals born with biological features of both sexes. Tragically, surgical "corrections" and concealment for people with ambiguous sexual identity have been standard medical practice since the 1950s. Surgeons simply retailored the genitals to look like one sex or another and collaborated with the family to keep the procedure—and the dilemma—a secret from the child. Medical wisdom (although in this case, medical ignorance might be a more appropriate term) forced parents into making a fundamentally important decision with far-reaching implications for the child, long before the latter had any ability to express an opinion, much less decide whether he or she wanted to be treated as a male or a female. Often, this met with disastrous results.

What should a parent do if they find themselves confronted with this predicament? Hazel Beh and Milton Diamond at the University of Hawaii have suggested that parents should manage the intersex condition *as a normal variation*. The child should have the situation completely explained to him/her, so there is no unnecessary confusion, guilt, or shame. Genital surgery can be dealt with later, when the individual child can communicate his or her own inclinations and participate in a decision to intervene.

This is not a book about intersex persons, but I have kept the idea of normal variations in sex at the front of my mind as I have worked on this book. For someone who is interested, as I am, in how we become male and female, the evidence that we have a sense of whether we are male or female *that cannot be manipulated after birth* is compelling. It's pretty clear that there is some indelible imprint on the human brain that creates and preserves in us an immutable sense of gender, in spite of external anatomy and environmental influences. ☙

Give your son a baby doll and encourage him (and his father) to play "Daddy" with it. (The worst thing that will happen is that it sits neglected with the wildly expensive toy he begged for as if his heart would break, and then never played with once.) Provide your daughter with balls and puzzles and lots of things with wheels. Mimi, one of my favorite 3-year olds, doesn't believe she's fully accessorized unless her purse contains both her cherry ChapStick and a Matchbox fire engine. As their interest in imaginative play develops, make sure your boy and girl children have equal access to pirate costumes, stethoscopes, and play kitchens.

The smart parents I know limit their children's exposure to media with an eye to stereotypes as well as sex, violence, and profanity. I think there's a great deal to be gained from watching TV with our kids and talking to them about what they've seen. (And because children are so heavily exposed to media in this country, they're expert media analysts by late childhood.) There's certainly nothing wrong with "Someday My Prince Will Come" if it sparks a conversation with Mommy about expectations and independence.

As parents, we have real opportunities to address some of the biases in society through the educational system. For instance, many parents and schools emphasize athletics for boys and downplay it for girls, despite the wealth of evidence that involvement in sports and physical activity is really good for girls, both physically and emotionally. That's an important bias to correct; insist on equal access to coaching, playing fields, and equipment at your child's school. While you're at it, take the family to a professional women's basketball game. It's fun, and tickets are still considerably less expensive than for the NBA.

The institutionalized bias against math and science for girls is also very real, and it's a particular thorn in my side. It is our job as parents to make sure that our daughters are offered the same opportunities as our sons. My own interest in science and medicine was fostered in my early life by my father, a doctor who would sometimes bring me on his rounds. Unfortunately, he did not support my decision to attend medical school. I did have the tremendous good fortune to be mentored there by a world-class scientist and doctor, one who happened to be a woman.

Those may have been different times, but I don't feel convinced that there is an equal playing field for girls in those disciplines. If your daughter shows an interest in these subjects (and, I would argue, even if she doesn't!) feed her what she needs to pursue it, from a chemistry set to arranging a tour of a real laboratory.

If you're a parent, it will probably seem perfectly natural to you that the next chapter of this book deals with stress. Certainly the stress of having, loving, and raising our children is one of the areas that causes conflict between men and women, but as we'll see, both sexes experience stress in fundamentally different ways—ways with a profound effect on the way we relate.

7

What's Wrong with Me?

Why Men and Women Respond Differently to Stress— And Why It Matters

I congratulated my patient Diane on being selected for a very prestigious Woman of Achievement award. Imagine my surprise when
this very powerful, self-possessed executive dissolved into tears in my
consulting room!

Her accomplishments had come at some personal cost. The constant
stress and competition had taken its toll on her sleeping habits and relationships. I wanted to talk about those issues, but instead, she seemed
fixated on a colleague of hers, a man who occupied a very similar position to her own in a different division of the company, and whose reaction to the pressure was diametrically opposed to her own.

"The tighter the deadline, the bigger the risk, and the greater the
consequences if we fail, the happier he seems to be. The stress is like
food for him. He thrives on it, while I feel utterly depleted by it," she
wept. "He makes me feel like I'm going crazy."

I was pleased to report to Diane that she wasn't crazy. Her impressions were correct:

Men and women *do* experience and react differently to stress.

Of course, our different experiences and reactions matter tremendously. We've all known (or been in) relationships that seemed as solid as bedrock until a variety of stressors closed in, squeezing us until we could barely breathe. Life, after all, is stressful—and now more than ever. Most American families struggle under tremendous pressure. We're worried about our personal health, about terrorism at home, about how we'll take care of our aging parents, about our children and what their futures hold. We work long hours and take very little vacation time, but it seems that no matter what we do, the wolf is never far from the door. We don't sleep enough or get enough exercise, leaving our bodies without the resources they need.

There are couples who can ride out such stormy weather—and, indeed, having a loving and supportive partner can be a true life raft in times of extreme strain. Why, then, does it seem that for the majority of people, stress is a profoundly alienating influence in our relationships, one that drives a wedge between us? When work is stressful, why do we find ourselves squabbling over who left the cap off the toothpaste? How does the same relationship that seemed like such a respite when we were lying on that tropical beach become a drain on our resources? Why do our partners so often seem like an additional burden, instead of a sanctuary where we can gratefully find refuge from the storm? And why are our relationships so taxed by the major events we go through together, instead of fuel for further intimacy?

Here again, I believe that the explanation lies in the differences between us. Stress, and all its manifestations, is different for men and women. The majority of the time, men and women are stressed about different things, and the concerns of the other person in the relationship can seem baffling and low-priority compared to our own. The way we experience stress is different, and the effect that stressful conditions have upon us, both physically and mentally, is gender-specific. Not surprisingly, the tactics we use to manage or deflect it are also different, and it is quite often the disparity between these strategies that gives rise to many of the conflicts that take place between us.

So again, given the differences between us, it's not a surprise to find ourselves on opposite sides of the fence when the going gets tough. It doesn't have to be this way. We can and should be one another's greatest allies and resources, especially when we're under pressure. It is my hope that a better understanding of what our partners think, feel, and experience when tensions rise can help us to use one another as bulwarks against inevitable outside pressures, as opposed to being the straws that break the proverbial camel's back.

Women Are More Stressed Than Men

A survey of more than a thousand adults commissioned by the National Consumer's League (NCL) in 2003 found that, as a group, Americans are stressed out. Thirty-nine percent of those polled said that work was a significant stressor in their lives; 30 percent cited family, 10 percent their health, and 9 percent the economy. (For most people I know, it's some combination of all four—plus wondering whether your dental plan will cover the work to fix your toothache, plus wondering how and when the broken hinge on the kitchen cabinet will get fixed, plus the nagging reminder that you owe your neighbors a dinner invitation, plus. . . .)

Younger people were more stressed than older generations, which is interesting (and in my opinion, a little sad), but I was most concerned by the noteworthy gender division. Women were significantly more likely to report problems and stress than men. Eighty-four percent of women, as compared to 76 percent of men, said that their stress level was higher than they'd like it to be.

What the two sexes were stressed about was different as well. Men—48 percent of them, as opposed to 32 percent of women—worried about work. Women—37 percent of them, as opposed to 21 percent of men—worried about family.

There are a million theories about *why* women are more stressed out than men. I suspect that much of it has to do with the multiple roles that women play. The women I know still assume the majority of the responsibility for their children and the home, regardless of how many hours they work outside of the home. If there is a breakdown in the system—a sick babysitter, for instance, or a leak in the basement—it's the woman who steps in to fill the gap. There appear to be protective benefits of these multiple roles—women who work and have a family seem to get less stressed out when something goes wrong in either place—but it leaves very little time for the kind of relaxation and downtime that our bodies and minds need to repair and recover.

The disparity takes a tremendous toll on our physical and emotional health. According to the NCL's survey, women are more likely than men to have experienced headaches as a result of stress. Perhaps more important, women are about two-thirds more likely to be depressed than men are, a truly staggering statistic about which I will write more in the next chapter. Researchers such as Kenneth Kendler, MD, who studies opposite-sex twins at Virginia Commonwealth University in an effort to discover why women are more prone to experience depression, has one possible explanation: While stress has a depressive effect on everyone, women are more likely to become depressed when exposed to much lower levels of it.

What Happens to Us When We're Stressed?

When a human being experiences stress (whether the stress is psychological or physical, as in the case of an injury or illness), we release a number of hormones designed to help our body cope. For instance, we manufacture adrenaline, the "fight-or-flight" hormone. Adrenaline interferes with our perception, so that we feel distanced from our surroundings, and everything seems to happen in slow motion. At the same time, it sends our blood pressure skyrocketing, so that our hearts hammer in our chests, our breathing becomes shallow and fast, and our senses are heightened (which is why a smell or provocative color can later trigger a flashback to a time of great stress).

We also release a hormone called cortisol, colloquially known as the stress hormone. One of cortisol's main functions is to regulate blood sugar. When it's released in stressful conditions, it both encourages your body to dump more energy into your bloodstream, while it encourages your cells to use less. Cortisol's role in regulating blood sugar explains the "I forgot to eat lunch!" phenomena that sometimes happens when you're under a great deal of pressure at work. It also explains why many people who spend their lives under constant stress are often overweight. Their bodies are continually trying to modulate their energy levels around the peaks and troughs in their blood sugar, brought about by cortisol's interference.

A little cortisol is a very useful thing. It helps the body to rise to the challenge of the stressor. But a lot of cortisol—the levels produced when we're under constant stress, for example—is much more debilitating. Cortisol attaches itself to cells in the body's immune system, hampering them from doing their jobs efficiently and weakening the overall system, leaving our bodies vulnerable to infection and disease. Researchers at Ohio State University found that stressors like an upcoming examination period slowed down the speed at which wounds healed in the mouths of students, and that women who were caring for relatives suffering from Alzheimer's disease healed more slowly than women the same age who were not.

It's not your imagination that you're more prone to sickness when you're feeling overextended. Your overburdened immune system can't rise to meet the additional challenge of a virus or infection. I got the flu for the first time in years the winter my mother died, even though I had faithfully gotten my vaccination. Uncharacteristically, it took me weeks to recover my usual good health.

Cortisol and Learning

Our cortisol levels fluctuate naturally over the course of a day, no matter what's going on in our lives. They're highest in the early morning and decline steadily as the hours wear on, so that they're lowest in the evening while we sleep. (They'll reverse themselves if you work the graveyard shift.) The fluctuations in cortisol that take place over the course of the day explain why many people (me included) do their best work first thing in the morning, when levels are highest, and find themselves fading mentally as the day wears on.

Cortisol is absolutely critical for learning.

People with insufficient cortisol have difficulty remembering what they hear, and people with too much of it (as when they're given a corticosteroid to control an illness, for instance) may also experience impaired mental ability.

Why is there such a strong connection between cortisol and learning? Because learning is the first step in creating memories, and we use our memories to avoid repeating experiences that cause us stress. You'll put your hand in the fire only once—the next time, the memory of the pain and the burn will stop you. In fact, as we discuss later in this book, there are special receptors for cortisol in the hippocampus, the part of the brain where we store memories, especially those associated with strong emotions (the memories we remember best anyway). It makes very good sense that we'd have a system for storing memories of the events that triggered the stress hormone!

While a little stress may promote learning, constantly high levels of it are extremely damaging to our cognitive processes. People with hyperfunctioning adrenal glands that produce too much cortisol all the time have smaller brains, and perpetually high levels of cortisol due to constant stress is also destructive to the cells in the brain. Our stress response developed to help us respond to sudden and emergent dangers, not the low-lying ambient threats of life in the 21st century, whether they're financial pressures or suicide bombers.

Brian Knutson, PhD, and his colleagues at Stanford University have evidence that chronic anxiety is associated with reduced brain mass in adults of both sexes and may play a role in creating the antisocial personalities of people who were seriously abused during childhood. Additionally, high levels of cortisol damage the part of the brain that stores memory, making it hard to learn new things and to remember old ones. This is why children with post-traumatic stress disorder have difficulty at school and why Vietnam combat veterans have trouble with both long- and short-term memory.

The Fear Control Center: The Amygdala

The production of adrenaline, cortisol, and all the other chemicals released by the brain under stress—the ancient systems in the brain so essential to our survival—is controlled by the amygdala, a walnut-shaped cluster of cells at the base of the brain. The amygdala also helps us to store emotionally charged experiences as memories, so that we're able to avoid or defend ourselves appropriately when the situation recurs. The hippocampus organizes a system of neurons that form a circuit that actually embeds a memory of the experience into our brains. In other words, the amygdala helps us to make the rich series of calculations that determine whether or not we should be afraid—and what we should do if we are.

For instance, the amygdala helps us to recognize facial expressions in another person and to use those to decide whether that person constitutes a real threat. Let's say that you and I are sitting in a room together when my laptop crashes. I mutter angrily, and you look at my face. Your amygdala helps you to interpret my expression as anger, but also to determine whether or not my anger poses a direct threat to you, based on the direction of my gaze. If I look angry, but I'm glaring at the blank screen of my computer, you might be concerned for its safety, but you can relax for your own. If, on the other hand, I'm glowering directly at you (perhaps because you borrowed my computer and opened a virus-riddled e-mail), your amygdala will trigger a fear response.

The amygdala acts as a watchdog, fortified with a whole retinue of memories it has endowed with an emotional load. These memories protect us from, or promote, our interaction with new experiences, based on what we already know and remember. We see the connection between fear and memory in monkeys whose amygdalae are destroyed. These animals have reduced fear when confronted with a new stimulus, because they can't test it against past experience. As a result, they'll explore and seek contact with a new object or person indiscriminately.

Why Women Experience Stress Differently

While the basic physiology of stress is similar for both sexes, there are some very important differences between the way men and women experience stressful events and how they remember them.

Let me illustrate with an example. There are two basic ways to react to a social challenge like entering a new room: You can "approach" the new environment (by walking up to someone who looks interesting and available for conversation and saying "Hi, I'm Marianne. Aren't the floral arrangements gorgeous?") or you can "retreat" (by lurking by the bar and waiting for someone you know to appear).

It was very interesting to learn that the two types of people actually have functional differences in the way their brains respond. People who reacted to social challenges by approaching the new environment activated the left half of the prefrontal cortex. By contrast, antisocial and shy people—"highly defensive" people—showed predominantly right-sided activation.

Now imagine the surprise of these scientists when they realized that this observation was gender-based. Their conclusions turned out to be true *only of men.* A fascinating new study showed that while shy and withdrawn men activated the *right* side of their frontal brains, shy and withdrawn women lit up on the left. Observations like these are so new that we have yet to completely understand what they mean for our function— in this case, how we perceive and respond to challenges. But certainly, we can conclude that the systems for responding to unpleasant events and encoding memories of them are quite different for the two sexes.

My patient Tanya provided me with a striking model of this phenomenon. She and her husband were mugged at gunpoint while returning from a late dinner. A year after the incident, Tanya was still experiencing nightmares and panic attacks, as if no time had passed. When I spoke to her husband to see if he was also suffering adverse effects, I found that he could barely remember what had happened. In fact, he had a considerably more accurate and detailed memory of his interactions with the police and the credit card companies than he did of the block of time when their lives had been threatened.

This might seem baffling—or fuel for the still-kicking theory that women are more prone to "hysteria" than men—but I think there's a simple, biological explanation. Let's look at some of the disparities in brain function between the sexes for help in explaining this.

You'll remember that women have more gray matter in the fronts of their brains, just behind the forehead. This prefrontal cortex area controls our decision-making processes and regulates our emotional responses to the world. It's this part of the brain that sends the messages to the hippocampus, where memories are made. During a stressful event, estrogen activates a wider field of neurons in this part of the brain, and estrogen levels are higher in women. *This means that women actually experience the unpleasantness in greater and more precise detail.* The mugging, in other words, was much more vivid for Tanya than for her husband, even though they were both there.

Women also produce more cortisol than men do under stress, and for a longer time. Progesterone, one of the sex hormones found in high levels in women, prevents cortisol from turning off. Since cortisol promotes learning and the formation of memories, these higher levels mean that women not only have a more visceral experience of the unpleasantness, but *we remember it better.* By contrast, the male sex hormone testosterone actually blocks the effects of cortisol.

Cortisol is just one factor contributing to our memory of an unpleasant event. Another has to do with our fear control center, the amygdala. Researchers have found a really interesting variation in the sexes: When making emotionally charged memories, men use only the right amygdala, while women use only the left. We don't know enough about this part of the brain to draw conclusions from this piece of news, but it seems certain from the little we do know that there's something there. For instance, scientists have found that smaller right amygdalae are found in people with a susceptibility to alcoholism.

The two sexes use different areas of the amygdala to influence memory. Women use the areas that connect to other areas in the brain, like the hypothalamus and the brain stem. The brain stem controls respiratory and heart rates. So particular circuitry may explain why women have a more urgent and physical response to emotionally charged memories. Men, on the other hand, use the area of the amygdala that connects upward to the more cognitive areas of the brain. This may mean that they form the basis for a more "rational," solution-based response to a challenge, like remembering to cancel the credit cards before your muggers get their new stereos.

Considering these differences in brain function, it's no wonder Tanya was still haunted a year later, while her husband could barely remember the outline of the events. I wonder if police officers are aware of these discrepancies as they collect eyewitness accounts and if their anecdotal observations would support the science.

Why would we evolve with different methods of coping with stress? From an evolutionary perspective, we have had different jobs. Viewed in that light, men's poor memory for the emotions they had during events loaded with danger makes sense. Let's say that the survival of our tribe depends on the hunting ability of the men. A good emotional memory is hardly advantageous to them: If they remember exactly how cold it was on the last mammoth hunt, how tired they were during the chase, how frightened they were, and how much it hurt when they caught a tusk in the thigh, how enthusiastic are they going to be next time? On the other hand, it's very useful for the women of the tribe, responsible for the care and well-being of the children, to remember that a favorite watering hole also attracts a number of frightening carnivores in the late morning, if that memory ensures that our paths don't cross again. Forgetting makes men brave, and for a very long time, that's what they needed to be.

Does Competition Work for Girls?

The differences between the sexes in the physiology of stress has called some of our most widely believed truths into question. For a long time, researchers concluded that competition promoted learning, but how we learn under stress may actually depend on our sex. Tracey Shors and George Miesegaes of the department of psychology at Rutgers University showed that exposure to sex-specific hormones, prenatally and after birth, was a crucial determinant of the impact of stress on learning in rats. Exposure to stress (a painful shock to the tail, for example) actually enhanced the speed at which male rats learned; they benefited from the pressure. The difference in females was vivid and startling: The ability of a female rat to learn was *impaired* when she was exposed to stress.

I once watched a teenage girl learning to drive in a parking lot. She was practicing turning right into a parking space over and over, while her frustrated father coached her from the passenger seat. Finally, near tears, she yelled at him, "Just leave me alone!" I ached to run over and share the results of this study with them. If those rats are any indication, she probably would have nailed that tight turn more easily if he'd given her a little space to breathe.

Further research suggests that these differences are hardwired. If you castrate a male rat at birth, his learning response will still respond positively to stress. On the other hand, giving testosterone to female rats at the time of their birth made their learning behavior exactly like that of males! If this pattern holds true in humans, it raises really important questions, especially for educators. It has long been believed that competition in the classroom prompts students to try harder and to push themselves, a theory that might work in favor of boys, but against girls. The observation that our sex hormones modulate learning during stressful experiences has important implications for women who are unhappy or anxious, like my executive patient Diane. To maximize her performance and her ability to learn and remember, Diane would probably benefit from removing as much stress from her environment as possible. Obviously, there's nothing that's going to make the working environment entirely stress free. (I even overheard a yoga instructor complaining bitterly about her clients and bosses—if that's not stress-free employment, then I'm fresh out of ideas!) But with a little planning and attention, I think Diane can make herself more comfortable.

To begin with, I encouraged her to investigate a better way of triaging the information that floods her office, so she doesn't feel as inundated. Just because she can multitask doesn't mean she should. Making a list of the day's tasks in order of their importance now helps her to keep on track and allows her to delegate many responsibilities to her able staff. I also thought that she'd probably see benefits from a regular lunchtime spin class or an after-work massage. And if she can't always control what happens in the workplace, she can at least make sure that she gets enough rest and relaxation on the weekends to make up for it. (Her nine-year old daughter *loves* going with Mom to get a manicure and pedicure.)

For her male colleague, on the other hand, if stress works as a motivator for him, it may benefit his performance—if not his overall health—to load it on.

Although a leap from animal experiments to conclusions about humans is always dangerous, the impact of stress on learning in rats raises some very interesting questions about hormones. Do post-menopausal women, with their lower estrogen levels, fare better than their younger colleagues under stressful circumstances—at least with respect to their ability to learn and remember things? Perhaps all Diane has to do to see an even playing field is to wait another 10 years!

How We Cope—And What Happens When We Can't

Although women experience more stress, and stress is more likely to lead to depression, women are actually more resilient to stress than men are.

It may be that women are relatively more hardy in the face of chronic stress or anxiety because they have more gray matter in the prefrontal area than men, giving them a "cushion" of extra cells that protect them. Additionally, estrogen neutralizes the damaging effect of a variety of stressors on neurons. This may help to explain why diseases like schizophrenia set in later in women than in men, why women react more quickly to lower doses of antipsychotic medicines than is the case with men, and why their profile of side effects from those medicines is different. (Estrogen and progesterone have an important impact on the way some drugs are metabolized in the liver). It's also probably why women retain greater intellectual ability and function as they age.

Women also have very different mechanisms for coping with stress. Men, famously, "go it alone," and they suffer from much higher percentages of stress-related disorders as a result. For instance, men are more likely to have high blood pressure and to abuse alcohol or drugs.

By contrast, women respond to stress by reaching out to other people, especially other women. They bond, they talk about their issues, and they recruit help. This response may not only help them to cope with the immediate threat, but protect them against the ravages of stress in general.

The groundbreaking research that gave rise to this discovery was done by Laura Cousin Klein, PhD, and Shelley Taylor, PhD, at UCLA. They noticed that women under stress were more likely to come in, clean the lab, and talk to other women; men, on the other hand, were more likely to seclude themselves. Since almost all of the research on stress had been done in men, there was no mention of this phenomena in the literature, which focused almost exclusively on the classic "fight or flight" response to a threat—the decision to confront a threat or to flee from it.

When confronted with a threat, men gird their nervous systems with the chemicals they will need to do battle or to run: adrenaline, noradrenaline, and cortisol. Their pupils dilate, their respiratory rates increase, and blood moves away from their digestive tracts and into their arms and legs in case they need to run. Their reflexes speed up, and their perception of pain diminishes.

Women have all these responses, but they tend not to utilize them. Why? Well, if you have young offspring, neither fight nor flight is a particularly good option. Fight, and you run the risk of injury, leaving you incapacitated and unable to protect your child. Flee, and you remove yourself from your home and systems of support, like a known food supply, and anyone who's traveled with an infant knows it can be hard just hailing a cab, let alone escaping during a real emergency. So women adapted to their circumstances by coming up with a different response, which Dr. Taylor and her team called "tend and befriend."

When a woman is under stress, her oxytocin levels rise. This not only calms her, but it prompts her to get help, in the form of bonding with others, especially other women. She has a much better chance of successfully protecting her young if she has access to additional re-sources—whether we're talking about food, money, childcare, or backup in a physical confrontation. Testosterone, as you know, coun-teracts the effects of oxytocin. This explains why men's response to danger or a threat is so different from that of women.

When I read about "tend and befriend," I was immediately re-minded of an event that happened to me many years ago. One after-noon, I picked up the phone and heard sobbing so intense that I thought I was dealing with a heavy breather. Eventually, through the sobs, I recognized the voice of a good friend. When she had finally calmed down long enough to talk, Stacey told me that her husband had contracted a sexually transmitted disease from someone he'd slept with on a business trip.

I said the most comforting thing I could think of under the cir-cumstances: "Say the word, and I'll be there in an hour. You and baby Emily can stay with us for as long as you need to. Everything you need is here." She declined with gratitude, we talked for a while longer, and I made an appointment for her to come to my office first thing the next morning for STD testing.

Over dinner, I shared the story with the man I was seeing at the time. He was unsurprised by the infidelity, but genuinely perplexed by Stacey's decision to reach out to another woman when she did. He claimed that a man would never have called in the heat of a crisis like Stacey did. "I can't imagine calling someone when I was still crying so hard I couldn't speak. It's completely unthinkable to me," he said.

His comment stayed in the back of my mind—until I found the ex-planation in Dr. Taylor's research. Stacey hadn't called me for help deciding what to do about her marriage, to explore her husband's motivation for cheating, or to complain about the ramifications of his irresponsible behavior (there were certainly plenty of those conversations later). She hadn't been calling to "chat"; there had been a real sense of urgency and emergency to the call she made to me. When I was describing it to my friend, I said that I felt a little like a 911 operator.

I believe that Stacey's call to me was a classic example of how women tend and befriend. Confronted with what must have seemed like a threat to her, she reached out to bond with another woman. And without realizing it (I had simply said the first thing that came to my mind, probably the thing that I would most have liked to hear in her position), I had fulfilled my end of the tend-and-befriend equation by assuring her that she could rely on me for protection and shelter for her and her baby.

As far as I'm concerned, tend and befriend is a wonderful example of the rewards we can reap if we simply take the time and energy to question the assumptions we've made on research done exclusively in men. Since I have learned about the tend-and-befriend phenomenon, I have seen interactions between women in a completely different light. All around me, I see women making alliances and realize how very powerful this is as a strategy for coping with stress.

So my advice to women, especially women under pressure, is to tend and befriend! Because while it's true that our natural impulse is to make connections with other women, modern life makes it hard. Think about how different your life would be if you lived with a number of other women. Don't feel like cooking tonight? Need someone to take a turn sitting with your sick baby? Need to borrow a book to match the particular mood you find yourself in tonight? These are pleasures almost forgotten, now that we no longer live in the same dwelling as our extended families. Additionally, there are a great many things competing with our time, making it harder and harder for us to form the bonds we need. But we've evolved with this potentially miraculous ability to thrive; it only makes sense to use it.

One of my oldest friends and I always have a terrible time finding a matching opening in our schedules for dinner, but we make the effort to do it, because even a quick bite to eat together is such a balm to our overworked souls. A glass of wine and some face time are just what the doctor (in this case, me) ordered to help us cope with the pressures of our lives, and we invariably leave refreshed and renewed, as if we'd taken a mini-vacation.

I have noticed an increasing reluctance, especially in younger women, to use the resources available to them. Like men, we think we should go it alone, and although there is much we can learn from our male counterparts, I don't think this is one of them. In fact, I'd like to encourage men to get in on the game as well!

Life is hard, and it's easier if you have help. A friend of mine with a new baby asked if I'd mind if she dropped by on a Sunday afternoon to return a recording she'd borrowed. When she showed up at my house, I saw she was dangerously exhausted and near the end of her tether. At my urging, she left the baby with me for an hour while she had a (solitary) cup of coffee and read the newspaper. When she returned, she was relaxed again and wonderful company for both me and her little one.

I see female medical students struggling alone when their studies and emotional well-being would surely benefit from the formation of a tutorial group. And I see my friends (and myself) canceling dinner dates with old friends when other responsibilities call. Women in particular have a regrettable tendency to drop all other relationships when they're in the throes of a new romance. How can you make time for Sunday brunch with old buddies when you're spending all your time staring into somebody's eyes? Such behavior isn't just rude, it's short-sighted. Your friends can ultimately mean the difference between navigating life successfully or sinking into real depression. So tend them well.

Men, probably because of their tendency to shoulder burdens alone, are much more likely to have high blood pressure and to abuse alcohol or drugs. They would do well to share their struggles with their friends—male or female—as women do. It's far healthier. Maintaining friendships that can help us to alleviate stress are as important a part of self-care as brushing your teeth or going for an annual physical. (You do go for an annual physical, right?) There's help out there; we simply have to ask.

Let us renew the social and family networks that comprise our most valuable fortifications against stress. Otherwise, we run the risk of depression, as we'll see in the next chapter.

8

What's Wrong with You?

Depression in Men and Women

Chloe is sure there's something wrong with her. If she isn't in my waiting room, she's on hold, waiting to tell me about a new symptom. In the past month, she has found lumps in her neck, skin lesions on her back, and a change in her sense of taste. With every symptom, the certitude that she's in the grip of a lethal illness guarantees that she'll have a debilitating panic attack.

None of Chloe's complaints seem to have a basis in reality, but she steadfastly refuses to address one that really does threaten her life: She is so thin that I am surprised her legs can support her. She exercises relentlessly for hours every day and monitors her caloric intake obsessively, while cooking large gourmet meals for her family and friends.

Another patient of mine, Adam, has a different set of problems. His work life is fraught with uncertainty, and he may be facing downsizing. But his behavior makes him very difficult to cope with these days. He can't stand loud noises and yells if the children play or even talk within earshot of him. He can't keep an assistant for more than a month because he berates them so severely for minor errors. He has begun to drink after dinner in order to sleep. And, in the incident that brought them to my office, he recently slapped his wife in rage and frustration when she accidentally knocked his glass off the kitchen counter. Although he'll admit to being more irritable than usual, he denies any feeling of sadness.

Both Chloe and Adam are suffering from the same mental disorder: depression. But this disease has many faces, and their symptoms are so different that the uninitiated physician may have trouble making the diagnosis. Some depressed people are so immobilized by panic attacks that it requires a prodigious act of courage for them just to leave their homes. Others complain of a profound feeling of unease and an air of unreality; they feel numb and untouchable, like they're in a dream. Some suffer from acute self-consciousness, coupled with crippling feelings of worthlessness, and others (mostly men) lash out. Some depressed people hurt themselves in an effort to control the pain they feel; others hurt themselves in an effort to end it.

Depression affects an estimated 19 million adult Americans every year. That means every single one of us will see our lives touched by depression, either because we suffer from it ourselves or because it affects someone we love.

Women and Depression

What does depression have to do with the differences between men's and women's brains? A great deal, when we look at who's afflicted by this disease: Of the 19 million Americans who suffer from depression, 12 million are women.

Women are overwhelmingly more prone to depression than men.

World-class authorities Jules Angst, MD, (I didn't make up his name) of the Psychiatrische Universitatsklinik in Zurich, Switzerland, and Dr. Myrna Weissman, PhD, of Columbia University, both have data that show that the gender ratio for depression is 2:1, with remarkable consistency, in at least 11 countries of the world. That's a staggering disparity, and one that we must begin to address.

I would like to insert an important note here about depression and men: I have long been convinced that depression is underreported, underdiagnosed, and undertreated in men, largely because of the way they're socialized.

Many men—especially those from less-enlightened generations—remember not being allowed to cry in pain or sadness, even as a very young child. In this day and age, boys are still taught not to complain, but to "suck it up" and to "stop whining." I think men are taught not to talk about the symptoms of depression, even to their doctors, and I think doctors—especially male doctors—often ignore the symptoms.

I casually mentioned my theory that depression in men is more prevalent than we think to a friend at a dinner party, and his answer chilled me to the bone. "Of course it's more common than anyone knows," he said. "It's why we die sooner than women do." There are correlations between depression and some major diseases, like heart disease and cancer. He may be more right than he knows.

My theories aside, both Dr. Angst and Dr. Weissman independently agree that the skew toward depression in women is real and biologically based. Women also experience depression differently: They get depressed at a younger age, they're more likely to also have panic disorder, and they report more physical symptoms, like fatigue and appetite and sleep disruptions.

The two sexes also "self-medicate" differently. Women often find that reward-seeking behaviors like shopping or eating can lessen depression temporarily. (One teenager, whose mother bought her a blouse she admired in an attempt to lighten her daughter's relentless sadness, became enraged when her mother gave her the gift: "You know that shopping is one of the only things that makes me feel better! If you were going to spend money on me, why didn't you let me do the buying?") Men, on the other hand, are much more likely to pursue antisocial behaviors, such as drinking or violence.

But why? Why are women so much more susceptible to depression than men, and what makes our response to it so different?

Nobody is quite sure. There's almost certainly not a single culprit, but instead a combination of factors, including our genes, our hormones, brain chemistry, and our roles in society. Let's take a look at how they each contribute.

Factor #1: Our Genes

There's quite a bit of evidence to suggest that depression has a genetic component. Avshalom Caspi, MD, PhD, and his colleagues at King's College in London published a remarkable finding showing that there is a specific gene with two different forms: one "long" and the other "short." People with the short form are more susceptible to depression after a stressful event than those who have the long type.

The mutations that make some vulnerable to depression, while others seem to sail through an identical experience unscathed, may have to do with the genes we have *because of our particular sex.* George S. Zubenko, MD, PhD, at the University of Pittsburgh in Pennslvania, and his colleagues have shown that there are at least 19 sites on our chromosomes that influence our susceptibility to depression. Several of these are linked with depression in women, more than in men. At least one sex-specific gene contributes to depression in men, but not in women.

This genetic factor may not only influence *who* gets depressed, but what they *do* in reaction to that depression. Not all depressives drink or use drugs, but some do become alcoholics and drug addicts. Why the disparity? This reaction may be genetically indicated. Other diseases, like heart disease and cancer, are also correlated to depression, if less directly. Might certain people be more prone to them because of their genes? The next generation of this research has the potential to help great numbers of people.

So genes are one factor contributing to depression. What else is there?

Factor #2: Our Hormones

Our susceptibility to depression is connected to our sex—but not just because of the chromosome our fathers gave us at conception. The genes that give us our sex also control the release of the hormones that continue to sex us over the course of our lives, making us more or less male or female. For instance, it's the Y chromosome, found only in men, that "tells" the body to produce testes, which in turn produce testosterone and other masculinizing hormones, turning a fetus into a little boy.

Our genes continue to regulate the release of sex hormones over the course of our lives, determining, for instance, how old we'll be when puberty sets in and how our bodies will react to the high level of hormones released then. Some boys, for instance, suffer from terrible acne as a result of the flood of testosterone that greets them at puberty; others escape with only the occasional blemish. Some become very muscular very easily; others never really escape their boyish bodies. The hormones are the same, but the genes that control them are responsible for the tremendous diversity between individuals.

What is the role of hormones in depression? If hormones can influence brain structure (and we've seen that they can), then might they not also influence our mood and our behavior? You don't have to look at research to know this is true—just ask any woman whose menstrual period is heralded by days of irritability, feelings of sadness, and sleeplessness, symptoms that occur when estrogen is at its lowest levels.

In fact, *fluctuations* in hormone levels might be the key to why depression is so much more prevalent in women than in men. There's quite a convincing argument to connect depression with these hormonal fluctuations when we look at the times in women's lives when they're most likely to be depressed—before their periods and after childbirth, to name two.

And since these fluctuations are unique to females—men's hormone levels stay fairly stable for most of their lives—they may explain the overwhelming predominance of female depressives.

The following stages are characterized by hormonal fluctuations and are strongly correlated to depression.

Puberty: At puberty, sex hormones surge in both sexes, leading to the development of secondary sex characteristics.

Then the paths diverge: In boys, testosterone secretion remains essentially stable after this initial sharp increase, while the production of ovarian hormones in a pubescent girl starts the cyclic pattern that will continue until she begins menopause. This cyclicity in women has im-

the data on the impact of these commonly used antidepressants during pregnancy are really quite reassuring. One recent study published in the journal *Lancet* showed that some babies do experience withdrawal symptoms—jitteriness—from SSRIs (drugs like Prozac), but the authors of the study acknowledge that maternal depression can also adversely affect the fetus.

When my depressed patients become pregnant, I always suggest that they have a serious conversation with their ob-gyn or midwives (and the prescribing psychiatrist, if there is one) about the pros and cons of staying on their antidepressant. This is really something that can be decided only on a case-by-case basis, with the patient as a full partner in the decision.

If the woman is adamant about stopping her medications, or if there is a medical reason to suggest it, I advocate that she and her doctors monitor her mood and sense of well-being very closely, and she gets help *at the very first indication* that a relapse is beginning. Even if medications aren't a possibility, there are other options. For instance, making therapy and counseling available (or more available) during the pregnancy can offset some very unpleasant and potentially worrisome months.

Postpartum depression: Another gender-specific example of the impact of changeable hormones is the depression that assaults some women after their babies' birth.

Virtually every mother has some period of depression during the first week or 10 days after delivery. I remember my husband's bewilderment at the attacks of sobbing I experienced the day after I brought my first-born home. Like puberty and the days before your period, this is a time of dramatically changing hormone levels. In the first weeks after delivery, estrogen levels drop suddenly, and since estrogen regulates neurotransmitter mechanisms in the brain, it may cause a sudden decline in those that regulate mood. (This is unquestionably exacerbated by the sleeplessness and general confusion that also distinguish this time.)

While most new mothers experience the baby blues at some point in the weeks after they give birth, these feelings usually go away. If feelings of depression and irritability continue and begin to interfere with her ability to function, then the new mother may have a serious condition called postpartum depression.

Few things are more frightening to new mothers—and their families—than this poorly understood and underdiagnosed disorder. It must be attended to, without fail. In severe cases of postpartum depression, a new mother can become psychotic; her risk of doing so is up to 20 times higher in the first month after her baby is born than at any other time in her life.

While postpartum depression can strike anyone, there's a greater likelihood that you'll experience it if you have a history of depression. About 33 percent of all women with postpartum depression and about 15 percent of those with postpartum psychosis have had similar episodes before pregnancy, as well as a family history of the disorder.

The mother is not the only one who suffers when postpartum depression hits. Susan Pawlby, PhD, from the Institute of Psychiatry in London, studied the children of women who were depressed in the postnatal period and found that the IQ scores of their 11-year-old boys was significantly lower (84) than it was in boys whose mothers weren't depressed (103) in the period after their birth.

Women with a history of depression should take special care when they get pregnant, especially in the vulnerable days, weeks, and months after birth. This disorder may not be entirely avoidable, but there are steps you can take to prevent it or to minimize its severity. For instance, women with strong social networks—relatives, friends, or other new moms who offer lots of help and companionship—are less likely to experience this disorder. Also, breastfeeding seems to have a protective effect. If you have a history of depression, you'll want to talk to your doctor about your options.

You must also ask your family to find out if your mother was depressed after you were born. I heard about a woman, 6 months into a terrible episode of postpartum depression, who discovered that her mother had actually been hospitalized for severe depression after her own birth. Of course, it wasn't diagnosed as postpartum at the time, and the family had kept the incident secret out of a misplaced sense of shame. To my mind, it's a double tragedy: Not only did her mother not get the treatment or understanding she needed, but knowing about this history might have allowed her daughter's doctor and ob-gyn to be more proactive about prevention and treatment.

Menopause: The brilliant Dr. Susan Love once called menopause the mirror of puberty: Our tissues and organs change shape dramatically once again, in almost a reversal of what happened to them at that earlier time. In terms of depression, menopause itself is usually not much of a problem, at least not long-term, but the years leading up to it (called perimenopause) can be a very different story. For many women, this process begins around 40, although it can begin earlier for some and later for others.

Here again, hormones play an active part. During the time leading up to the actual cessation of menstrual periods, a woman can experience dramatic ebbs and surges in her hormone levels. Production is unsteady: Some months, she'll ovulate, which raises her estrogen and progestin levels; other months, her pituitary gland pummels her ovaries with follicle-stimulating hormone in vain, and her levels sink again.

Since estrogen is strongly connected to the proper functioning of our brains, a falloff in its level can have a profound effect indeed. I have menopausal patients whose ability to think clearly is so impaired (one patient calls it "fuzzy brain") that they are convinced they are losing their minds and wonder if they shouldn't be tested for Alzheimer's disease. They lose their car keys, eyeglasses, and everything else that isn't attached to them, and they can't remember names of places and people they've known all their lives.

This can be deeply and profoundly upsetting, setting the stage for a major depression. One particularly brilliant executive who runs an entire department of people in a massive, multinational corporation was so terrified by the change in her mental abilities that she considered suicide until we urged her to take estrogen. It completely restored her to normal, and she simply laughs at any suggestion that she should stop, even after the bad press hormone therapy has received over the past few years. She says (with some intensity) that she'd rather be dead than give it up.

As with pregnancy and postpartum depression, it's hard to isolate specifically what's hormonal and what can be attributed to other factors. Many women do get depressed with the onset of menopause, because of what they feel it means. Some describe feeling "dried up" and old; others mourn the loss of their fertility (even if nothing on earth could convince them to go through teething and colic again). Our culture puts a tremendous premium on youth, and it can sometimes be hard for women to understand that they're not leaving the pleasures of their youth behind. Other well-documented symptoms of menopause include weight gain, a decrease in sex drive, and fatigue—all elements that can spark or worsen a nascent depression.

Factor #3: Our Brain Chemistry

As do genes and hormones, actual differences in the chemistry of the male and female brain may also play a part in the greater incidence of depression in women. For instance, men make 52 percent more serotonin than women and have higher levels of serotonin in their blood than women. This may be at least part of the reason depression is more frequent in females than in males.

It's probably not the whole picture, though. A short few years ago, we were enchanted with the connection between defects in neurotransmitters and depression, but now, the picture is much more complicated. We're beginning to look at the ways cells "talk" to one another: Their messages travel along a sort of highway system we call the signaling pathway. Our ideas for better treatment of depression and other mental illnesses will focus on this signalling pathway to determine how disordered thinking, mood disturbances, and even psychoses can be prevented and corrected.

Factor #4: Our Roles in Society

There are striking differences in the characteristics, incidence, and symptoms of depression in men and women. I'm convinced they are rooted just as importantly in the way we are treated by the societies in which we live, as by true biological differences between our brains.

In the last chapter, we learned that men and women cited different issues as the primary stressors in their lives: work for men, family for women. Given the close connection between stress and depression, it's not surprising that we get similar results when we ask why the two sexes get depressed. Both sexes in Dr. Angst's survey reported stress as a cause of their depression, but males were more likely to cite physical illness, work problems, and unemployment as precipitating causes.

I mentioned previously that there's no difference in the rate of depression between girls and boys before puberty—a good indication that hormones are one of the culprits behind the discrepancy in depression rates. But some experts don't believe that hormones play a significant role at all. Benjamin Hankin, PhD, and Lyn Abramson, PhD, psychologists at the University of Wisconsin, ascribe higher rates of depression in pubescent girls to societal treatment rather than physiology, pointing out that girls are more likely to experience negative events like sexual abuse than boys and also are more dissatisfied with their body shape and physical appearance than boys.

I don't fully agree with this. The hormonal changes are significant, and while there is a tremendous amount of pressure put on young women to look a certain way (i.e., thin), I'm not sure that it's as restricted by gender as the authors of this study would have us believe. Ask the mother of any adolescent boy—especially one who's overweight or shorter than his classmates or late to develop the deep voice and musculature of his classmates—and she'll tell you that boys have their own issues with body image. One of my adolescent patients weighed more than 200 pounds at the age of 15. He looked at me before he got on the scale and muttered sadly, "I am a sow."

But there is certainly a societal component to explain why women get more depressed than men do. The conflicts and pressures of puberty are a heavy load to carry for a young girl. And because this may be the easiest factor to address, we owe it to the girls in our society to do what we can to lighten that load.

Motherhood appears to be another significant factor in women's depression. Professor M. Lucht and his colleagues in Germany surveyed more than 4,000 residents of Luebeck and found that motherhood seems to have a profound effect on risk for depression: It more than doubled in women who had children.

These results beg important questions about the modern world. Would teenage girls be so susceptible to depression if the culture they consumed focused more on developing their social awareness and intellect, as opposed to a concave belly and finding the perfect cropped shirt to show it off? Would motherhood be so strongly correlated to depression if it was viewed as a more significant accomplishment by a more supportive society and if so many women weren't doing it in isolation?

Shopping, Snorting, and Smoking: Addiction, Depression, and Sex

Janet is the darling of the salespeople at the high-end clothing boutiques near her office. They call her whenever a new collection comes in and get word to her secretary that a "pre-season sale" is about to take place. Often after buying one or two items she really likes, Janet surveys the store for others, until she's convinced she has everything in her bag that she might remotely want. Usually she carries even huge bundles directly home; she can't wait for UPS to deliver in a few days, and she even fantasizes that her purchases will be damaged or lost if mailed.

Janet knows she's an object of ridicule for one or two of the people who wait on her. If she disciplines herself to make a choice between two things—perhaps different only in color—the one she left behind will inexplicably creep into her consciousness and stay there until she calls up and orders it. (Knowing her pattern, the salesperson will often already have put it aside for her.) Every once in a while, a responsible retailer will tell her that she doesn't need what she's about to buy. But Janet's purchasing isn't about need or the things themselves; it's about the pleasure-seeking circuits in Janet's brain.

Janet is addicted to shopping—in the same way that another person might be addicted to a drug like cocaine or to smoking or to compulsive overeating. All these addictions are "reward-seeking behaviors" and involve dopamine, the chemical in the brain that stimulates pleasurable feelings through special receptors. To keep feeling the high, an individual has to engage in more and more of the behavior. Lower-than-normal numbers of these special receptors seem to be a common denominator in addictions of all kinds.

Is a poverty of these receptors a *consequence or a cause* of excessive or addictive behavior? We simply don't know. But if we could help Janet stimulate dopamine with activities other than shopping, we might have the key to much more effective treatment programs.

Like all addictions, Janet's shopping doesn't happen most when she's feeling down, as you might think it does. In fact, the excitement of her complex and challenging work pushes her into a kind of hyper-excited state in which she is driven to more and more pleasure-seeking behavior—a kind of this-feels-good, I-want-more-of-it cycle. But that doesn't mean there isn't a strong link between the way she behaves and an already existing depression.

As I've learned to expect, the studies on addiction and addictive behavior have been done almost exclusively on men. But it's time for a change: Addictive behaviors are prevalent and very destructive among women. Adolescent girls and young women become addicted to drugs and alcohol more easily than males and at lower doses than their male counterparts. Women now make up almost 40 percent of the drug-addicted population, with devastating consequences: Nearly 70 percent of AIDS in women is related either to their own use of intravenous drugs or to having sex with an infected drug user. Drug use during pregnancy is linked to small head size, low birth weight, stroke, and Sudden Infant Death Syndrome (SIDS).

The scientists at the National Institutes of Health (NIH) have become aware of how damaging it has been to restrict clinical studies only to men, so they're taking initiatives to sponsor research on women. The result is that the National Institute of Drug Addiction is expanding its gender-specific research agenda. I will be the first in line to read the results of the gender-specific studies currently under way at the NIH. Certainly, what we already know about the difference between men and women (and, tragically, boys and girls) and addiction suggests that there are substantive differences in the reasons behind male and female addiction and the effects of that addiction on the brain.

Different Motives

Boys and girls may begin using addictive substances for different reasons. Girls often experiment with smoking and alcohol to medicate stress and depression, sometimes as a consequence of having been sexually abused. Dr. Dean Kilpatrick of the Medical University of South Carolina is studying a national sample of 4,000 women to explore the link between drug addiction and the experience of violent abuse such as rape, sexual molestation, physical assault, or natural catastrophes—all of which can be the basis for post-traumatic stress disorder (PTSD). The extraordinary youth of the women when the crimes were committed against them is appalling: Six out of 10 rape victims were not even 18, and 29 percent of girls were raped when they were younger than 11.

PTSD sufferers were almost four times as likely to have major alcohol and drug abuse problems than those who had suffered similar violence but who didn't meet the criteria for PTSD. When compared to the normal population, PTSD sufferers were 10 times more likely to have alcohol-related problems and 17 times more likely to have drug abuse–related problems. By contrast, boys often start drugs, including alcohol, in a thrill-seeking mode or as a way to solidify their social position among peers.

There is a substantial connection between drug and alcohol abuse and other self-abusive behaviors. In girls, there is a highly significant connection between substance abuse and eating disorders. An important 3-year study of addicted females—headed by Joseph A. Califano Jr., chairman of the National Center on Addiction and Substance Abuse at Columbia University—observed that half of individuals with eating disorders abuse alcohol or drugs, compared with 9 percent of the general population, and 35 percent of abusers have eating disorders, compared with 3 percent of the general population.

Different Treatments

Differences in addiction—why people become addicted and what happens to their brains in response—are worth studying because they will help us to help people to quit. In fact, the addictive intensity and the motivation for using illicit substances for men and women are so different that many treatment services have established separate rehabilitation programs for the two sexes.

Certainly, treating depression—to which women are twice as susceptible—may help. In fact, one way to successfully treat addicts is to treat the depression that drives them to pleasure- or reward-seeking behaviors. Experts at Stanford University Medical Center tried a commonly used antidepressant, cialopram (Celexa), on compulsive shoppers and found it to be so effective that not only the problem shoppers but the investigators themselves were amazed at the results.

In a study at McLean Hospital in Massachusetts, more women were diagnosed as having major depression than men and responded only for a short time after being hospitalized. Women's symptoms improved much more slowly than those of men after they stopped using the prescribed antidepressant. Men, on the other hand, improved steadily for the 4 weeks of the study, and their eventual functional recovery was superior to that of women. The study investigators thought this might have been due in part to a sense of hopelessness and distress that was more profound in women, largely because of their more dire financial situation; many had to cope with simply finding enough money to get by.

Reproductive hormones also make the impact of drug abuse on men and women different. For example, testosterone appears to be protective against the effects of cocaine. Normal female rats and castrated male rats needed much lower doses of cocaine to exhibit the same changes in behavior that noncastrated males needed for a similar effect, and castrated newborn males and newborn female rats given testosterone at birth both needed higher doses of cocaine than normal animals later in life, in order to produce an effect. So the men in the McLean study may have recovered better because their brains were protected from the effects of the drug by their higher levels of testosterone.

Estrogen has a slightly different protective effect. Marc Kaufman, PhD, of the Brain Imaging Center at the McLean Hospital in Massachusetts found that in a group of 24 healthy males, a dose of cocaine, which is a powerful constrictor of blood vessels, reduced blood flow to the brain. The degree of vasoconstriction was dose-related. In a second study, he looked at the effect of cocaine on both sexes. In that study, Dr. Kaufman found that women *didn't* have a reduction in blood flow to the brain if they used cocaine during the estrogen-rich phase of their monthly cycles. After they ovulated, though, the same amount of cocaine produced a 10 percent decrease in their brain blood supply.

In any case, the women were still better off than men, who showed a 20 percent reduction in brain blood supply on similar doses of the drug. The vasoconstrictive effect of cocaine is probably the cause of the cumulative effects of its use on cognition. There is subtle but real brain dysfunction in about 80 percent of long-term users, and it doesn't go away during periods of abstinence. The protection estrogen offers helps to explain what we've known for some time: Women have less brain damage from chronic cocaine abuse than men.

Dr. Kaufman thinks that estrogen administration might give a useful boost to drug-rehabilitation strategies—even for men. He may be wrong about that, though. Two groups of scientists have found that estrogen actually increases the stimulant effect of cocaine in rats. Others have noted the longer and more intense high that women report after snorting cocaine, compared with that of men. The findings suggest that women may exhibit more intense drug-seeking behavior than men and, like the laboratory animals, quickly increase the amount of cocaine they use if given the opportunity to do so. That wouldn't be surprising. We know that estrogen keeps "feel-good" dopamine-associated neurons healthy. Without estrogen (and after menopause), the population of these neurons diminishes quite rapidly.

Quitting Smoking: Different for Men and Women

If I was given an influential soapbox, I would use it for one thing alone: to implore every single smoker out there to quit. Did you know that women are 20 times as likely to get lung cancer from cigarette smoking as men? As with all addictive behaviors, different strategies may be required to get men and women to quit.

A recent French study found that men needed higher doses of nicotine replacement to quit smoking successfully than women did, and that men who got higher doses of the nicotine were more likely to quit than men on lower doses. Women did not achieve greater success when the dosage was increased. So when my male patients are trying to quit, I encourage them to get enough nicotine replacement.

Female vulnerability to cigarette addiction may actually be established in the womb. The daughters of mothers who smoked when they were pregnant are more likely to become smokers themselves than other girls; this is not the case for boys.

For women, quitting smoking seems to be more complicated than simply replacing the chemical. I have given worry beads, semiprecious stones strung on a silk cord, to a number of female friends as they embarked on their journeys to quit smoking. Different types of stones feel different. Amber is always warm and slightly sticky, and the beads tend to hold onto the fingers, while crystalline stones like jade are cool and smooth and offer no resistance at all. Women, sensitive as they are to touch, find such aides very helpful in quitting. They help to console the quitter for the loss of the accoutrements of smoking—the matchbook cases, the cigarette cases, the holders, the lighters, and other beautiful objects associated with the vice.

Women also continue smoking because it's a way to control their weight. Metabolism is set higher by nicotine, and weight gain after giving up cigarettes is common. If that's going to be a significant obstacle when one of my patients wants to quit, I refer her to a nutritionist *before* she starts her renunciation campaign.

How We Treat Depression in Men and Women

Men and women have different strategies to cope with depression, and their doctors should too.

Contrary to what the drug companies would have you believe, there's no magic "happy pill." It's not as easy for us to treat depression with medications as you might think. Many patients need trials on several different kinds of medicine before hitting upon the right one.

Often, a medication that has worked for a while stops working; this can be very disruptive, as can the process of finding a new one.

Men and women also respond differently to antidepressant medications, something most people don't know, and I think this is still not sufficiently taken into consideration when doctors are prescribing. For instance, young women are more sensitive to side effects like excessive fatigue on very small doses of medication. Some of these may be due to the effect of estrogen on the brain or to sex-specific ways of metabolizing these medications.

Which drugs work may also be sex-specific. Robert R. Bies, PhD, at the University of Pittsburgh has shown that depressed men with anxiety attacks respond to the older generation of tricyclic antidepressants, such as imipramine (Tofranil), better than women, but women seem to do better with monoamine oxidate inhibitors (MAOIs), such as Parnate.

The fact that men make and metabolize more serotonin may explain why Paxil—a drug that prolongs the amount of time that serotonin lingers in the synapse between neurons—works better in women than in men. The difference in response may also be due to a difference in the numbers of receptors for serotonin in the brain between the sexes. There are fewer binding sites for serotonin on men's blood cells' platelets than on women's.

Something Must Be Done

It should be clear to you by now that we don't have a complete picture to explain why women and men suffer depression at such different rates.

What we do know is that this disease has far-reaching effects. Mark Whisman, PhD, and Lauren Weinstock, MS at the University of Colorado studied 774 married couples and found something devastating:

The level of anxiety and depression *in each spouse* predicted not only their own marital satisfaction, but their spouse's as well. Depression influenced both husbands and wives more than anxiety in how they felt about the marriage.

Additionally, the children of depressed mothers are more likely to have behavioral problems, developmental difficulties, and social problems and are themselves more prone to depression than their peers. So when someone is diagnosed with depression, mental health evaluations *for the whole family* should be the very next step.

The discovery of some basic physiological differences between men and women has helped us to become better doctors and to give better, more individualized care to our patients. Learning the differences between men's and women's hearts made us better cardiologists. The same *must* be true about studying the brain in order to improve what we know about and how we treat mood disorders such as depression. Because this disease has such far-reaching effects, it is absolutely imperative that we do what we can to establish why these differences exist and how they might be remedied.

9

Where Did I Leave My Keys?

Men, Women, and Aging

"He's making me nuts." Julia runs her hands through her short gray hair. "He follows me around the house like one of those terrible little dogs. I can't get anything done! Was he always this dense? It seems like I have to explain everything 40 times."

Julia is a longtime patient of mine, in for an annual checkup. Her physical health is terrific, but as I'm hearing, her mental health is something else entirely. The source of the strain: her recently retired husband. "Thirty years, two kids—we spent so much time talking about how great it would be for him to be out of the rat race, but I'm spending our retirement doing everything I can not to kill him!"

Unfortunately, Julia is hardly alone. Many people (and their spouses!) find the "golden years" of their retirements a surprisingly bitter pill to swallow, and I can't count the number of stunned patients

I've seen, struggling to figure out why they're not happy now that they've gotten this long-awaited treat. Once again, I suspect that the answer lies in the significant differences between men and women— and in this case, in how they age. As I explained to Julia, while men and women both get older and experience physical, mental, and sexual changes as a result, the process manifests itself differently—*and with different timing*—in both sexes. Ultimately, we become more like each other than we have been at any other time in our lives since childhood, but getting there can be rocky. The differences between us can cause a great deal of conflict—just as life is supposed to be getting much easier.

The Aging Brain

We're living longer than we ever have before; in fact, our life spans have doubled in the past 100 years. Retirement used to signal the end of a productive life; now it's quite literally a third act, filled with travel, the satisfaction of long-postponed creative impulses, new loves, and second (or third) careers. This third act will be enjoyed by record numbers. By 2050, $\frac{1}{5}$ of the American population will be 65 or older.

With so many more happy, healthy, active older people, our conception of aging is evolving as well. The AARP was recently up in arms about an ad for a cell phone that would make it easier for the elderly to get in touch with their "doctors and grandchildren." I teased one of my older patients about it when I saw her answering her e-mail in my waiting room; she smiled up at me, thumbs still flying over her slender platinum handheld, and hummed, "Times, they are a-changing."

Aging seems to be a double-edged sword. On the one hand, I don't agonize over every reversal or disappointment the way I did when I was 20; they don't seem to have the same intense weight they used to. A missed telephone call from the man of the hour doesn't precipitate a crisis, and if my son forgets he agreed to have dinner with me, I shrug it off, happy to see that his life is full and busy too. Things don't seem to be as catastrophically important as they once did, either. I find I lend my daughter my favorite clothes and jewelry without even a twinge of anxiety, and a worn spot in a wonderful Oriental carpet merely reminds me of how many times I have happily walked through my beloved apartment.

But that's not all that's changed. I have to pay attention when I put my house keys away, so I won't spend 15 minutes looking for them the next morning. I now have to remind myself to focus on what I'm doing, so I don't get hopelessly distracted by one of the other thousand things that I'm processing simultaneously. It's harder for me to learn a new song at my piano, and I absolutely cannot remember the name of a novel I loved 10 years ago.

My male friends have different complaints and celebrations, but certain things are the same. Our more fixed abilities, like our vocabularies, deteriorate less than more sophisticated processes like our ability to show good judgment or the capacity to pay attention to what we're doing. As we'll see (and you will eventually!), the memories of both sexes are particularly susceptible to the ravages of time.

Let's look now at the differences in the way we age and how those differences affect us and our relationships.

Scheduling Conflicts

Many of the "symptoms" of aging—both the good and the bad—have to do with a change in brain function, largely because of the change in the amount of hormones we release at this time in our lives. Of course, men and women release different hormones in different amounts at different times, which is one of the key reasons that there is such a disparity in the way we age.

We shouldn't be nearly as surprised as we are that we age at different rates and in different ways. We know that men's and women's brains develop on different schedules from the very moment of conception, and much of this has to do with the different schedule that both sexes have for the production and release of the hormones that make us male or female.

For instance, in the male fetus, testosterone secretion is high—levels equivalent *to that of an adult male*—in gestational weeks 8 to 24 and for the first 6 months after birth, after which the levels fall. By contrast, ovarian secretions are low during the intrauterine life of a baby girl, but they are significantly higher during the first 6 to 12 months after birth. Roslyn Fitch, PhD, and her colleagues at Rutgers University have summarized the extensive evidence that ovarian hormones play a role in tailoring the female brain—but with different *timing* than occurs with testosterone in the male.

Levels of these hormones continue to differ throughout childhood, with great effect on the brain. As you may remember, one of the major processes through which our brains develop is called pruning, the programmed cell death of millions of connections in the brain. Neuroscientist Patricia Kuhl, PhD, has shown that pruning is one of the major factors in how we develop language, for instance. Babies from homes where English is the primary language learn to distinguish the sound "r" from "l" at around 6 months (to hear the difference between the words "rake" and "lake," for example). All babies—no matter where they are born or what language their parents speak—are born with the ability to differentiate these sounds, *but the connection has to be used.* Since no such distinction exists between these sounds in Japanese, a Japanese baby's brain will have "pruned" out this skill by the time she is a year old. What you don't use, you lose. Some child development experts suggest that pruning back unused neurons actually strengthens synapses between the cells that are left, making them more elaborate—in the way that you cut roses back to encourage new growth.

The different sex hormones influence how—and when—our brains do this pruning and weed out the connections that don't get reinforced by stimulation. This tailoring process happens on a different schedule for girls and boys from childhood through adolescence. One of the reasons for this is that estrogen seems to delay the systematic destruction or "pruning back" of "extra" cells, which is so important for brain maturation.

Additionally, there are major differences in the *timing* of pruning, brain growth, and the numbers of connections made between the two halves of the brain in boys and girls. A very interesting study from the National Institute of Mental Health showed that gray matter in the frontal part of the brain increases just before puberty, but at different ages (at 12.1 years for boys and 11 years for girls), then declines in both sexes. Increase in the gray matter of another part of the brain, the parietal lobe, was also earlier for girls (peaking at 10.2 years, contrasted to 11.8 years for boys).

This difference in the impact of hormones on brain architecture may help to explain the different pace of the development of skills in adolescent boys and girls. I attended an 8th-grade graduation last spring and was stunned by what I saw: The girls looked like self-possessed young women, while the boys looked like—well, boys. (A mother with two older sons confirmed my observation, saying simply, "This is always a big summer for the boys.") Planning and judgment—relatively advanced functions that depend on a developed cerebral cortex—appear earlier in females than males, although there may not be any significant difference in these skills by the time both are fully grown.

The hormonal differences between us continue over the course of our lives, although the next time they're as dramatically altered as they are during puberty is when we get older. Women cease to menstruate, and their levels of hormones like progesterone and estrogen decline. This is called menopause, and it typically happens between the ages of 45 and 60, although it can come earlier for women with

To Replace, or Not to Replace: For Her

Many women have abandoned hormone therapy (HT) as a result of recent data from large studies that showed that HT in postmenopausal women can cause early and harmful effects in a small subset of the population. But there is an enormous amount of information to show the beneficial effects of estrogen on neuronal structure and function.

A study showed that postmenopausal women who are on estrogen therapy have relatively more blood flow to the hippocampus—which is pivotally important in memory formation—than women of the same age who are not on estrogen. Sally Shaywitz, MD, and others make a very persuasive case for using estrogen to preserve and promote cognition and memory. Dr. Shaywitz points out that we need to clarify estrogen's role in cognition because the symptoms that older women experience of memory loss often have a powerful and devastating effect on the quality of their lives. It may not seem like a big deal to misplace your glasses, but when it happens 10 times a day, it represents a huge waste of time and can significantly erode your confidence. Similarly, forgetting the name of someone you've done business with hundreds of times can be very damaging to a relationship. These "small" lapses don't seem so small when they're happening!

Dr. Shaywitz has shown that estrogen can help. It alters brain activation patterns in postmenopausal women in the regions of the brain that are associated with the kinds of memory function we call upon in daily life—like remembering telephone numbers that we've just looked up, for example. The estrogen given to the women in her experiments reinstated patterns of brain activation characteristic of younger, premenopausal women.

Dr. Shaywitz's work is exciting for a number of reasons. I am entranced by the idea that brain organization is not fixed as we age, but can be changed some diseases or for those who have had surgery affecting the reproductive organs.

Symptoms of menopause vary. Some women have an extremely unpleasant time of it, while others hardly notice. We've discussed some of the psychological repercussions in Chapter 8, but there are some very real physical symptoms as well, including hot flashes, night sweats, itchy skin, breast tenderness, vaginal dryness, weight gain, an increase in allergic symptoms, fatigue, a lessening in libido, memory lapses, and incontinence.

back to the more effective circuitry we used as younger females. In some ways, this study prompts more questions than it answers; the participants did not show any change in the performance of memory tasks, possibly because the period of observation was very brief. But it is an exciting avenue to explore, and we will surely hear more about this in the future.

Although Dr. Shaywitz is careful to note that the decision to take estrogen is a personal one and should be made in concert with your doctor, the data seems to be an argument in favor of HT. Certainly, many women in my own practice and others maintain that their memories, ability to solve problems, and concentration have returned to normal since they've begun hormone therapy.

So, in spite of the apparently damaging implications of the results from recent studies, there will probably be a return to the judicious use of HT in older women. The specific purpose would be to preserve and/or restore intellectual abilities, with the added benefit that HT stabilizes mood and restores beneficial sleep patterns.

Hopefully, as we develop more and more sophisticated techniques for documenting the positive effects of estrogen on brain anatomy and function, we will also learn how to select the women who will benefit most from HT after menopause. There are other options, as well. For instance, we may have to explore variations of the estrogen molecule, so that we find a way to get the benefits without the risks of the native hormone.

In my opinion, the abundant evidence that replacing estrogen preserves and promotes an optimal state of brain function makes it a compelling candidate for use in some form in older females. ⌒

One of the most profound symptoms of menopause is clouded thinking. Patients describe feeling fuzzy or easily confused; others experience memory lapses ranging from the comical to the terrifying. Because estrogen has a protective effect on neurons, some of these symptoms may be relieved through hormone therapy, but it's not a perfect choice for every woman (see sidebar on page 204 for details).

Women are not the only ones who suffer from a decline of gonadal hormones as they age—and, with it, suffer hot flashes, night sweats, disturbed sleep patterns, increased irritability, a decline in memory, and problems with concentration. Men do too—yes, even the hot flashes. It's been variously labeled andropause, Androgen Decline in the Aging Male (ADAM), and even Partial Androgen Deficiency in the Aging Male (PADAM).

There *are* differences between the male and female versions of this "pause"—primarily, that women experience a decline in hormones over a compressed time in our lives, while for men, the falloff is more gradual. But there are a great number of similarities too, and it can be very useful for men (and the partners who live with them) to know a little bit more about this stage of life.

The most common complaints of men who felt they had entered andropause were erectile dysfunction (46 percent), general weakness (41 percent), and memory loss (36 percent). As he ages, a man will become more sensitive to pain, which testosterone seems to protect against. His physical strength will decrease unless he works on fitness consistently and carefully. Just as yours, his special senses of sight, hearing, taste, and smell will all become less acute, adding to his general fragility and tentativeness.

To Replace, or Not to Replace: For Him

Hormone replacement for the aging male has not been as rigorously examined as it has in women. Whether it will cause more harm than it will remedy is really not established at this time.

Most doctors believe that decreased testosterone is responsible for the changes in libido and erectile function in older males. Aging men whose testosterone levels fall also exhibit decreased muscle mass and strength, fatigue, depression, irritability, and diminished mental acuity. And that's why doctors have concentrated on replacing testosterone.

So here's the million-dollar question: Does testosterone replacement help memory loss in aging men with low testosterone levels? In one study, healthy older men (between 50 and 91) with cognitive problems had an improvement in working memory when they were given testosterone for 3 months. Another study showed no effect of testosterone on memory loss, although visual-spatial skills do seem to improve with testosterone.

There are cons to replacing testosterone, and treatment has to be watched very carefully. Testosterone increases the numbers of red blood cells (which may make blood much more viscous), depresses high-density lipoprotein levels (good cholesterol), and possibly damages the liver. Sleep apnea can also be made worse. Most important of all, prostate size can increase to a dangerous degree, and undetected prostate cancer can be made worse by hormone treatment.

Testosterone isn't the only hormone that begins to decline. Others include: the growth hormones dehydroepiandrosterone (DHEA) and dehydroepiandrosterone sulfate (DHEAS), insulin-like growth factor-1 (IGF-1), as well as hormones produced by the thyroid and the kidney.

There's been a great deal of press about DHEA in particular, called by enthusiasts the elixir of youth. Unfortunately, the data are not persuasive, although two studies did show some benefit from oral DHEA replacement. In one, a study of 20 adults who ranged in age from 40 to 70, 3 months of daily treatment produced an increase in well-being but did nothing for sagging libidos. ⌐

The consequences of the andropause can be grim, not only for the men who experience it, but for their wives as well. One thing to be vigilant for—whether you're an aging man or his spouse—is the onset of depression. A lessening in capabilities and erectile dysfunction can seriously erode self-confidence and self-esteem. Men also tend to define themselves by the work they do, and the loss of that definition when they retire can be extremely disorienting and have a depressive effect.

To make matters worse, retirement often forces couples into closer proximity than they may have been during all of their married lives. I asked Julia when she last had to share domestic space around the clock with her husband, excepting vacations. "When the kids were born, maybe?" she strained to remember.

For the rest of their lives, Julia's husband would get up, shower, eat breakfast—and leave the house for 9 hours, leaving her blissfully alone to get the kids off to school and then write the parenting articles that have made her reputation. Now, he's following her around the house.

It's natural to be at a loss as to how to fill the sudden gift of idle hours that retirement brings, especially if you're someone who's always suffered from too little free time. One patient told me she'd taken to inventing at least one errand a day for her husband that would take him out of the house so she wouldn't go completely mad.

Julia's husband eventually settled into a routine. He exercises every morning. He has become active in an organization that works to conserve Central Park and is considering a bid for the board. He has a quick lunch once a week with their grown son, a luxury he never had the time for before this. And he is learning to cook, which Julia suspects will eventually lead to an updated kitchen—a project she's more than happy to let him spearhead.

The Incredible Shrinking Brain

The brain gets smaller with age, but the loss of tissue isn't uniform, and it differs, depending on whether we're male or female.

Investigators are just beginning to look at these differences and to speculate on what they might mean. So far, they don't always agree. The Gurs and their colleagues at the University of Pennsylvania Medical Center in Philadelphia studied adults ranging from 18 to 80 and found that the left side of the brain atrophies more than the right in men. The left hemisphere matures later in boys than girls, and the Gurs think that the brain regions that mature last may also be the ones most vulnerable to deterioration as we age. These are the areas involved in decision making and judgment, which may explain the tendency of older people to "dither" rather than make quick, decisive changes in their routines and lives. In women, the change in brain volume is symmetrical and less pronounced than that in men.

Why do women lose less tissue? It may be because they have more blood flow to the brain, which offsets the cognitive effects of aging. It may also have something to do with the protective influence of estrogen on brain structure and function (and provide a powerful argument for the use of estrogen therapy in postmenopausal women to preserve their intellectual function). Whatever the reasons, the Gurs suggest that women may have less age-related change in mental abilities than men because their brains are slower to atrophy.

The changes in men's brains begin much earlier than in women— and earlier than we had suspected: Between 18 and 45 years of age, men show significant decline in their cognition, while women of the same age (presumably because of the protective effect of estrogen) do not show any change. After 45, the rates of decline seem to be quite similar in both sexes.

What are the implications of this greater (and earlier) loss of tissue in men? Researchers believe that it may explain some of the differences we see between the sexes as they age. For instance, men may suffer more profoundly and earlier from the loss of left-brain functions such as the construction of speech and the interpretation of language. The Gurs also believe that the loss of tissue in the left frontal cortex may explain why men are so much more likely to buy a red convertible or sleep with a much younger woman during a midlife crisis. It's this part of the brain that thinks about consequences and provides self-control. Possibly in an effort to compensate for loss of left-brain substance, we know now that men have more active metabolism in the right half of their brains as they grow older, while it stays more evenly distributed in women.

The activity of other parts of the brain changes differently in a sex-specific way with age too. The hypothalamus is the area that controls such varied and essential tasks as the regulation of appetite, sexual behavior, body temperature, endocrine activity, and emotion. Metabolism in this area of the brain is higher in older women than in men.

On the other hand, men have more activity on both sides in the thalamus, the brain's "air traffic control center," which identifies and sorts incoming sensory signals and transmits the information to the appropriate areas of the cortex. This may account for the difficulty older women have in concentrating—why so many of us forget what we've entered a room to fetch, for instance, or forget where we've put something. My patients tell me that they have "too much on their minds," but I blame the subtle and progressive disintegration of the thalamus. The amount of information pouring into the brain is the same, but they have lost some of their ability to triage it, so that they can exclude stimuli that's irrelevant to the task at hand.

We see differences in activity in other parts of the brain as we age as well. The cingulate gyrus is an essential part of the brain's executive function: It helps us to assess the consequences of our actions—and to change our activities accordingly. For example, if a task we are doing is difficult and complex, the cingulate gyrus helps us to slow down and be more careful, or even to try another strategy if the one we've devised isn't working. When this area isn't working properly, several disorders become apparent. Some people may try to correct problems that actually don't exist. In obsessive-compulsive disorder, for example, a patient may check something over and over again, like whether or not he has turned off the stove or closed the garage door properly. Alternatively, if this center is underactive or inadequate, a person may not be able to recognize mistakes and correct them, as happens in mental disorders such as schizophrenia.

Research shows that cingulate gyrus activity lessens more with age in men than in women. Our aging husbands or fathers may make mistakes in judgment more frequently as a result of this gender-specific difference in activity.

Communication Malfunction

With age, communication between the two halves of the brain decreases. This happens earlier in men than in women, who retain language skills at least until menopause, when their estrogen levels begin to decline.

Talking across the hemispheres, which occurs through the huge interconnecting highway between them called the *corpus callosum,* is important to understanding the unspoken components of conversation, like tone of voice or the facial expression of the speaker. Women experience a decline in this ability at the time of menopause, which may be related to the fact that women listen with both sides of their brains (unlike men, who use only the left side). Defects in women's right brains are apparent by the time they reach the 55–60 age group.

This limitation may be one reason why women in this period of their lives "take things the wrong way." They may understand the words but not the *intent* of the speaker. After a lifetime of translating nonverbal forms of communication to supplement the words they hear, the dulling of this ability can leave women feeling awkward, like fish out of water.

Memory Loss, Alzheimer's, and Dementia

Any discussion of aging naturally brings us to one of the biggest paradoxes in modern science. We have essentially doubled life expectancy since 1900, when the mean duration of life was only 48 years, but we don't know how to preserve brain function in our oldest patients, even if they are in optimal physical health.

By the ages of 90–100, almost everyone has significant problems with thinking and remembering how to complete even the simplest routines of daily life. Melissa Gonzales McNeal, MS, and her colleagues at the Oregon Health Sciences University found in a study of 100 healthy adults older than 85 that by the time we reach a mean age of 97, 65 percent of us will have what scientists call cognitive impairment (a general term for forgetfulness and the inability to concentrate, solve problems, and deal with the ordinary challenges of self-care). By age 100, almost half of us (49 percent) will have Alzheimer's disease, one of the severest forms of cognitive impairment.

Although women retain more brain function later in life, once it goes, it really goes. Women have a higher risk for Alzheimer's than men, age for age, and may be more susceptible than men to dementia. (It's also worth noting that Alzheimer's doesn't just affect women in greater numbers because we're more likely to get it. We're also more likely to end up taking care of someone who has it, like a spouse, a parent, or a sibling.)

Why do women seem to be more prone to dementia? Researchers have proposed the following:

Loss of brain mass: Women may lose less brain mass than men do, but they also start out with less. Since women begin with fewer neurons than men, the loss of even one neuron may be relatively more important than for a man. The greater interconnectedness of neurons within the female cortex may also explain why women are more susceptible to the dementia of aging. Like one bulb going on a string of Christmas lights, the loss of one neuron has a widespread effect on others. Men's more centralized processing may contain the damage.

Longer life span: Part of the problem may also be that women live longer. Men are more vulnerable to disease and early death than women are, with the result that by age 85, women outnumber men *2 to 1,* although we started out life in approximately equal numbers. (When young women tell me "there are no men out there," I tell them they're sitting pretty compared to their widowed grandmothers.) It's possible that the men who have managed to survive to "old—old" age (a new phrase coined at the NIH) are more fit and sound than the rest of their sex. In any case, by the time we're over age 85, women are more likely to have problems with thinking compared to men—the few who are left to keep us company.

Hope for Interventions

We don't know why dementia strikes. So much threatens our brain cells: accumulation of damaged (oxidized) molecules (scientists call this the "oxidative stress of aging"), inadequate energy supplies, mistakes in the production of new proteins because of gene mutations, insufficient blood supply, and those are just a few of the most obvious challenges.

There's hope, though. The more we learn about the brain and aging, the more apparent it becomes that the brain has a remarkable ability to *preserve* neurons in many areas and *to compensate for the loss of neurons* by increasing the connectivity between remaining neurons.

We seem to be very resourceful creatures. As the frontal lobes of our brains shrink, we seem to recruit other areas of the brain to help us carry out the higher functions they once controlled. A study done on a group of people in their 20s and 30s showed that they used their frontal lobes for tasks that required memory and the organization of information. Older people used a different part of the brain usually involved in registering and processing visual information. Young and old did equally well in learning and remembering a list of words that they had to organize into categories and recall accurately.

Additionally, neuroscientists are concentrating on interventions that can combat the changes in our brains that may give way to dementia. For instance, we know that the brain contains stores of stem cells that can—under the right circumstances—divide and differentiate into functioning neurons. One of these warehouses is located in the hippocampus, the part of the brain that we use for spatial learning and short-term memory. Aging subjects often show shrinkage in this part of the brain and will often have problems in recalling pictures of common objects or in navigating a maze seen the previous day. (As you may remember, chronic stress is deadly for the hippocampus and for memory; prolonged exposure to high levels of the "stress hormone" cortisol destroys cells in this part of the brain.) So facilitating the right circumstances for those cells to turn into working neurons may mean that we can regain some memory and spatial function.

There are also growth factors (chemicals that actually promote the formation of new cells) that promote neuronal survival in the brain and may increase the connections between nerve cells, for example. Other researchers are exploring the role of a class of substances called *chaperone proteins* (I thought that was a charming name), which ensure the proper configuration of the large protein molecules produced in the brain and oversee the destruction of damaged proteins. And perhaps unexpectedly, caloric restriction can also prompt the formation of new brain cells.

Medications are another option. For example, a medicine that improves the activity of a particular chemical called protein kinase A in rats improved the animals' memories. But stimulating the very same chemical in the frontal cortex actually impairs certain kinds of thinking, so the problem is complicated. Doctors are exploring the use of medications that suppress cell death, including cholesterol-lowering statins, which have a direct action on neurons. One day, we may have vaccines that prevent degenerative brain conditions like Alzheimer's; these are already being developed.

But these are all in the future. As Paula Bickford, PhD, at the University of South Florida Center for Aging and Brain Repair in Tampa warned in a recent interview, so far, no drug has been developed that really improves memory in humans.

What Can You Do Now?

Thankfully, not all solutions are out of reach.

In spite of all the criticism of hormone therapy (HT) for postmenopausal patients, estrogen is an important element in keeping the brain intact and neuronal performance optimal. The pendulum may swing back (as I think it will) to the *early* and careful use of HT in the postmenopausal patient. Once degenerative diseases such as Alzheimer's are well-established, though, hormone therapy may not have any effect on reversing or even slowing its progress.

If we've learned anything from Eric Kandel, MD, professor at Columbia University College of Physicians and Surgeons in New York City, it's that the brain is plastic and dynamic and contains the ability to change. Much has been made of providing very young babies with a variety of gentle sounds (including conversation), different textures, sensations, and environments to encourage the growth of their brains. As a result, toy companies have expanded their wares so that it's hard to find a baby gift that doesn't purport to make the little one smarter.

While the elderly too need to "use it or lose it," there's no industry rushing to their aid. Enriching the environment of older people and encouraging them to exercise *can actually induce the formation of new nerve cells.* I was very moved by a recent description in the *New York Times* of the interaction between a terminally ill nursing-home resident and the sympathetic visitor assigned to keep him company. The story was a remarkable account of how conversation and exposure to such things as literature and complex music increased both the patient's interest in life and his ability to recall memories and produce a progressively richer vocabulary and flow of speech.

I cannot emphasize enough how important it is to keep your brain well nourished with good music, good art, good conversation, and good ideas. The richer the environment in which you live, the greater the chances of increasing the number of, and connectivity between, your brain cells.

Even if you've begun to have some intellectual difficulties, there's a very good chance these problems can be fixed. The Seattle Longitudinal Study of Adult Intelligence, a massive study that followed more than 5,000 people for more than 4 decades, has shown that those difficulties can be reversed. An educational program significantly improved the thinking of two-thirds of the people to whom it was given, and 40 percent were restored to normal functioning!

Intellectual stimulation, while important, isn't the whole picture. Contact with others is part of a healthy environment. Don't overlook the importance of physical contact. Like babies, we need to be touched and will wither away without it.

Here are some suggestions to help you keep your brain in tip-top shape.

Eat well and exercise (yes, the sweaty kind). The brain, like every other collection of cells in the body, benefits from good nutrition. It can't do what it needs to do without the proper fuel! Appetite does dwindle as we get older, though, and buying and preparing healthy foods can take low priority, especially if we're alone. It's essential to eat healthily, including low-fat, high-protein meats and a variety of fruits and vegetables. Take a daily multivitamin. Ask your doctor if any of your health conditions, such as hypertension or heart disease, might benefit from a dietary approach as well, and if the instructions are unclear, ask for recipes.

New research shows that aerobic exercise can also protect the brain from the ravages of age. In one study, physically fit adults retained more brain density—specifically in the areas of learning and memory—than sedentary ones.

Learn a new game. Preferably choose one that exercises your brain, like bridge or chess. My family plays a game of Scrabble at almost every holiday gathering, and I treasure the conversations that take place over the board as much as the knock-down drag-out wordplay.

Do brainteasers. Try serial subtracting (start with a random number, say 1,356, then subtract 8, then subtract 8 from that answer and keep going) or create lists of words that mean the same thing (beautiful, gorgeous, lovely, stunning, etc.). Crossword puzzles, jigsaw puzzles, logic puzzles all work. What you do doesn't have to represent a major time commitment, but doing a little something every day can help.

Write your history. One of the best ways to exercise your memory is by remembering. Make your personal history available to other people. The project can span your whole lifetime or an important episode: meeting and dating your spouse, life during wartime or after terrorism, or the arc of your professional career. If you do write it down, consider giving bound copies as a wonderful holiday gift for family members. And if writing doesn't appeal, consider videotaping or audiotaping memories for posterity.

Take a class. There are ample educational opportunities for older people in most communities, ranging from current events discussion groups and technology seminars to jazz appreciation and food-tasting tours in ethnic neighborhoods.

Volunteer. Most of us wish, over the course of our lives, that we had more time to give back to the community, but work and children can make it hard for us to share our gifts as generously as we'd like. Seize this opportunity and reap the benefits yourself as well.

Sex and the Older Person

When I asked an elderly patient if she was sexually active, she laughed and asked me if I were testing her remote memory. But the problems that the sexes encounter in the bedroom as they age are real and are no laughing matter.

A recent survey, put out by University of Chicago sociologist Edward Laumann, PhD, (and sponsored by Pfizer, the company that makes Viagra), showed that many older women may be coping with partners who suffer from sexual dysfunction. Of the nearly 28,000 men and women over the age of 40 in 30 countries who were surveyed, 20 percent of men over 40 said they suffer from erectile dysfunction. Dr. Laumann also found that men became sexually dysfunctional twice as quickly as women did as they aged.

This can have extremely detrimental effects on a relationship. Men, in an effort to work on their erectile dysfunction, may demand new, imaginative, and time-consuming efforts from their wives in bed. One patient of mine told me, to her enormous chagrin, that she felt as though she had become a "sex object" to her recently retired husband. Other men, angry and humiliated by the lack of cooperation from their equipment, may freeze their wives out altogether—hardly a satisfactory solution.

Men may be having technical difficulties, but women didn't fare much better in Dr. Laumann's survey. Apparently, 31 percent of women over 40 have a low interest in sex, and 21 percent do not enjoy it—including 14 percent who find it painful. Depression and other psychological factors diminish people's interest in sex after the age of 40, and diseases like diabetes and hypertension also contribute.

It's not your imagination. Sex does change as you get older. With the decrease in estrogen that comes with menopause comes a reduction in sensation, particularly in the vagina, clitoris, and perineal area. This decreased sensitivity can affect how easily you become aroused and how easily you achieve orgasm. The vaginal walls may become less elastic, thinner, and drier.

You may also feel less sexy, with the result that you feel less like having sex and less adventurous in the bedroom. I can't overstress the importance that self-image plays in our understanding of ourselves as sexual beings. This is especially true for women. Although some older women say that they've never been so relaxed or felt so liberated about sex, we're presented with tragically few images of older women as sexy or desirable—with the result that sex can feel like a party you're no longer invited to.

There are a few things you can do to ensure that you continue to feel sexy and desirable.

Work out. Strength training has many physical benefits (muscle strength and an increase in bone density, to name two), but it may also help our sex lives as well. The first benefit is in how you see yourself. When you're fit and strong, you feel better about yourself because you look better and because your body is performing better. Strength training may also increase testosterone levels, which can naturally boost your sex drive.

Eat healthily. Many women gain weight with the onset of menopause. It's worth it to stay vigilant against this, and not simply for aesthetic reasons. Being overweight is linked to a host of medical problems, including hypertension, heart disease, diabetes, and joint problems—all of which can, in turn, interfere with a happy sex life. If you make an effort to stay at a healthy weight, you'll not only look better (and feel sexier), but you'll stick around longer to collect the rewards.

Stay hydrated. One of the sexual problems older women report is a lack of lubrication. Staying well hydrated by drinking lots of liquids will help. I do recommend that my patients supplement with artificial lubricant if moisture is a problem. (These range in texture and feel; it may behoove you to experiment with brands until you find one that feels "natural" to you and your partner.)

Talk to your partner. Let him know what's going on! The same things that have made you very happy in the past may not work anymore; you may need more stimulation now or a different kind or more time. It will certainly make him feel better when he understands that you're less sensitive because of changes in your hormone level, not because you're less attracted to him or because he's "lost his touch." And the two of you can experiment together to find satisfying solutions.

Masturbate. If you don't have a partner—or one whose company you enjoy in bed—that doesn't mean that you have to give up sex entirely. Masturbation can help to keep your sexuality alive and well until a partner comes along—or not.

Conclusion

Brain science is one of the most explosive and rapidly expanding areas in gender-specific medicine. It's tremendously exciting to stand at the threshold and to imagine what the future holds. I, for one, would like to know definitively whether the differences I've observed in the behavior of men and women—whether in my own personal life or in 30 years of listening to patients and students—have as much of a basis in sex-specific biological differences as I think they do. The research I did for this book convinces me that this will turn out to be the case, even though we aren't always sure yet what the new information means in terms of human behavior.

Does unearthing a biological basis for the differences in our responses and fundamental behaviors change our relationships? Of course—it happened to me while writing this book! I'm not just a researcher and doctor, but a woman. And in the past year or two, because of my work on this book, I see male-female battles through a new filter. Knowing why certain behaviors happen has helped me enormously (and the men in my life as well); I feel much more forgiving about things that might have made me angry a year ago and better able to communicate my own needs and desires. Simply put, knowing more about how we work—and how we work together—helps. Knowing the "why" behind the things that drive us crazy (whether with irritation, affection, or lust) can equip us to behave better with one another. (It surprised me a little that knowing more hasn't simply helped me to navigate the rough patches, but the great times too. You might think that it would "kill the buzz" to know that all those delicious sensations we associate with falling in love are the result of a chemical cocktail, but I have found the exact opposite to be true.)

The reaction of my patients to this material has convinced me that I'm right. They say that hearing about the differences and speculating how they might impact the behavior of both sexes has made them feel enormously hopeful. They can deal much better with the relationships in their lives if they have some explanation for things that seemed incomprehensible to them before, and they're jumping at the chance to implement real-life strategies that take advantage of this new research. In fact, one of the most gratifying parts about writing this book was watching my assistant apply what she learned to her own marriage— to the point where she was sometimes waiting for chapters as they came out of the printer! It's my hope that you too will feel both more understanding, and better understood, after reading this book.

But the most exciting thing for me to come out of the research I have done on this book is the world of possibility promised by the work of the great Eric Kandel. Like the lowly sea slug, I can not only learn from the men in my life, but my brain can actually change as a result. I love knowing that I can change my attitudes and responses to be more like theirs at those times and in those places where they can show me a more successful approach. Likewise, they can—and must, I think—learn from me.

This is already happening as both sexes, in increasing numbers, go to places traditionally closed to them before: men to careers that they can pursue at home while taking an active role in raising their children and women, who now have unprecedented educational and vocational opportunities, to a wide variety of jobs outside of the home. Traditionally all-male provinces, from exclusive prep schools, to golf tournaments, to stock car racing, are opening up to women, while more men are finding satisfaction in those domains that used to be open only to their wives.

If experiences literally change the structure and chemistry of the brain, we are going to become more alike one another. We are already learning from one another—more rapidly than we've ever done before. I believe that the incredibly adaptable brain will reflect this much more even playing ground, so that over time men's and women's brains will become more alike. Learning useful and effective strategies from one another puts our relationships on better footing because the communication between us gets easier.

With the knowledge that our brains can change comes a very important responsibility. If similar opportunities and even-handed treatment by the societies in which we live will improve the relationships between men and women, then we must make sure these opportunities are available to all. We're not ready to rest on our laurels quite yet; there's still quite a bit of work to be done.

It's an exciting time to be looking at the impact that sex and gender have on the brain. Men and women are already more alike than they are different, and it's my very firm conviction that we are becoming even more so. But there are differences between us, important differences that we should not hesitate to investigate and to celebrate. As the wonders of the brain in all of its miraculous complexity become clearer to us, we shouldn't fear the differences we might find, but instead we should seek them out and explore their implications for how we behave and how well we deal with the world around us. I, for one, am looking forward to seeing what happens when we do.

Notes and References

Introduction

p. xix. Godwin, J., Crews, D., and Warner, R.R. "Behavioural Sex Change in the Absence of Gonads in a Coral Reef Fish." *Proc R Soc Lond B Biol Sci.* 1996. Dec 22:263(1377):1683–8.

p. xix. "The Way of All Fish" is one of three separate miniplays in *The Power Plays,* written by Alan Arkin and Elaine May.

p. xxii. Committee on Understanding the Biology of Sex and Gender Differences. "Exploring the Biological Contributions to Human Health. Does Sex Matter?" Theresa M. Wizemann and Mary-Lou Pardue, Editors. Board on Health Sciences Policy. Institute of Medicine. National Academy Press. Washington, D.C. 2001.

Chapter 1

pp. 4–5. Kandel, E.R. *Cellular Mechanisms of Learning and the Biological Basis of Individuality in Principles of Neural Science.* Third Edition. Eric R. Kandel, James H. Schwartz and Thomas M. Jessell, eds. Elsevier. New York. 1991. p. 1028.

p. 7. Raisman, G. and Field, P. "Sexual Dimorphism in the Preoptic Area of the Rat." *Science.* 1971. 173:731–733.

p. 8–9. Dabbs, James McBride. *Heroes, Rogues, and Lovers.* McGraw-Hill. New York. 2000.

p. 9. Gur, R.C., Turetsky, B.I., Matsui, M., et al. "Sex Differences in Brain Gray and White Matter in Healthy Young Adults: Correlations with Cognitive Performance." *J Neurosci*. 1999. 4065–4072.

pp. 9–10. Gur, R.C., Gunning–Dixon, F., Bilker, W.B., and Gur, R.E. "Sex Differences in Temporo-Limbic and Frontal Brain Volumes of Healthy Adults." *Cereb Cortex*. 2002. 12(9):998–1003.

p. 9. Chaugani, H.T., Phelps, M.E., and Mazziotta, J.C. "Positron Emission Tomography Study of Human Brain Functional Development." *Ann Neurol*. 1987. 22(4):487–497.

p. 10. Joshua Rubinstein, PhD, of the Federal Aviation Administration, and David Meyer, PhD, and Jeffrey Evans, PhD, both at the University of Michigan, describe their research in the August issue of the *Journal of Experimental Psychology: Human Perception and Performance*, published by the American Psychological Association (APA).

p. 11. Kulkami, J. "Gender Differences in the Quality of Life of People with Schizophrenia." Presentation at the 1st World Congress on Women's Mental Health. March 27–31, 2001. Berlin, Germany.

p. 11. Bornheimer, B. and Diethelm, A. "Psychiatric Home Treatment—A New Service Preferably for Women." Presentation at the 1st World Congress on Women's Mental Health. Berlin, Germany 2001.

p. 11. Huber, T.J., Schneider, U., and Emrich, H.M. "An Open Prospective Study of Estradiol Levels in Schizophrenia and Related Disorders" (abstract 310). *Archives of Women's Mental Health*. 2001. 3 (suppl 2):71.

p. 11. Davis, K.L., Kahn, R.S., Ko, G., and Davidson, M. "Dopamine in Schizoprenia: A Review and Reconceptualization." *Am J Psychiatry*. 1991. 148:1474–1486.

p. 12. Greenough, W.T., Black, J.E., and Wallace, C.S. "Experience and Brain Development." *Child Develop.* 1987. 58:539–559.

p. 12. Bornstein, M.H. "Sensitive Periods in Development: Structural Characteristics and Causal Interpretations." *Psychol Bull.* 1989. 105:179–197.

p. 12. DeBellis, M.D., Keshavan, M.S., Beers, S.R., Hall, J., Frustaci, K., Masalehdan, A., Noll, J., and Boring, A.M. "Sex Differences in Brain Maturation During Childhood and Adolescence." *Cerebral Cortex.* 2001. ll:552–557.

p. 13. Gron, G., Wunderlich, A.P., Spitzer, M., Tomczak, R., and Riepe, M.W. "Brain Activation During Human Navigation: Gender-Different Neural Networks as Substrae of Performance." *Nature Neuroscience.* 2000. 3:404–408.

p. 14. Saucier, D.M., Green, S.M., Leason, J., MacFadden, A., Bell, S., and Elias, L.J. "Are Sex Differences in Navigation Caused by Sexually Dimorphic Strategies or by Differences in the Ability to Use the Strategies?" *Behav Neurosci.* 2002. 116:403–410.

p. 14. Gur, R.C., Alsop, D., Glahn, D., Petty, R., Swanson, C.L., Maldjian, J.A., Turetsky, B.I., Detre, J.A., Gee, J., and Gur, R.E. "An fMRI Study of Sex Differences in Regional Activation to a Verbal and Spatial Task." *Brain and Language.* 2000. 74:157–170.

p. 14. Christiansen, K. and Knussmann, R. "Sex Hormones and Cognitive Functioning in Men." *Neuropsychobiology.* 1987. 18:27–36.

p. 14. Halpern, D.F. *Sex Differences in Cognitive Abilities.* Third edition. Mahway, NJ: Lawrence Erlbaum Associates. 2000.

pp. 14–15. Ehrhardt, A.A. and Meyer-Bahlburg, H.F.L. "Effects of Prenatal Sex Hormones on Gender-Related Behavior." *Science*. 1981. 211:1312–1317.

p. 14. Berenbaum, S.A. "Cognitive Function in Congenital Adrenal Hyperplasia." *Endocrinol Metab Clin North Am*. 2001. 30:173–192.

p. 15. Spencer, S.J., Steele, C.M., & Quinn, D.M. "Stereotype Threat and Women's Math Performance." *Journal of Experimental Social Psychology*. 1999. 35: 4–28.

Chapter 2

p. 19. Federman, D.D. "Three Facets of Sexual Differentiation." *New England Journal of Medicine*. 2004. 22:350(4):323–4.

p. 30. Cary, M.S. "The Role of Gaze in the Initiation of Conversation." *Social Psychology*. 1978. 41(3)

p. 32. Perper, T. and Weis, D. "Perceptive and Rejective Strategies of U.S. and Canadian College Women." *Journal of Sex Research*. 1987. 23, 455–480.

p. 44. Karama, S., Lecours, A.R., and Leroux, J.M. "Areas of Brain Activation in Males and Females During Viewing of Erotic Film Excerpts." *Hum Brain Mapp*. 2002. 16(1):1–13.

p. 47. Basson, R. "The Female Sexual Response: A Different Model." *J Sex Marital Ther*. 2000. 26:51–65.

pp. 49–50. Carmichael, M.S., Humbert, R., Dixen, J., Palmisano, G., Greenleaf, W., and Davidson, J.M. "Plasma Oxytocin Increases in the Human Sexual Response." *J Endocrinol. Metabl*. 1987. 64:27–31.

p. 53. Kayner, C.E., and Zager, J.A. "Breastfeeding and Sexual Response." *J Fam Pract*. 1983. 17:69–73.

Chapter 3

p. 62. Pillips, M.D., Lowe, M.J., Lurito, J.T., Dzemidzic, M., and Mathews, V.P. "Temporal Lobe Activation Demonstrates Sex-based Differences During Passive Listening." *Radiology*. 2001. 220:202–207.

p. 68. Ragland, J.D., Rand Coleman, A.R., Gur, R.C., Glahn, D.C., and Gur, R.E. "Sex Differences in Brain-Behavior Between Verbal Episodic Memory and Resting Regional Cerebral Blood Flow." *Neurophysiologia*. 2000. 38:451–461.

p. 75. Christiansen, K. and Knussmann, R. "Sex Hormones and Cognitive Functioning in Men." *Neuropsychobiology*. 1987. 18:27–36.

Chapter 5

p. 108. Weeks, David and Jamie James. *Superyoung: The Proven Way to Stay Young Forever*. London: Hodder and Stoughton. 1998.

p. 122. Baker, B., Paquette, M., Szalai, J.P., Driver, H., Perger, T., Helmers, K., O'Kelly, B., and Tobe, S. "The Influence of Marital Adjustment on 3-year Left Ventricular Mass and Ambulatory Blood Pressure in Mild Hypertension." *Arch Intern Med*. 2000. 160(22):3453–8.

p. 129. Najib A. *American Journal of Psychiatry*. December 2004. 161: 2245–2256.

Chapter 6

p. 137. Alexander, G.M. and Hines, M. "Sex Differences in Response to Childrens' Toys in Nonhuman Primates (Cercopithecus Aethiops Sabaeus)." *Evolution and Human Behavior*. 2002. 23(6):467–479.

Chapter 7

pp. 159–160. Wu, H., Wang, J., Cacioppo, J.T., Glaser, R., Kiecolt-Glaser, J.K., Malarkey, W.B. "Chronic Stress Associated with Spousal Caregiving of Patients with Alzheimer's Dementia is Associated with Downregulation of B-lymphocyte GH mRNA." J Gerontol A Biol Sci Med Sci. 1999. Apr:54(4):M212–5.

Chapter 8

p. 178. Caspi, A., Sugden, K., Moffitt, T.E., Taylor, A., Craig, I.W., Harrington, H., McClay, J., Mill, J., Martin, J., Braithwaite, A., and Poulton, R. "Influence of Life Stress on Depression: Moderation by a Polymorphism in the 5-HTT Gene." *Focus.* 2003. 3: 156–160.

p. 183. Sanz, E.J., De-las-Cuevas, C., Kiuru, A., Bate, A., and Edwards, R. "Selective Serotonin Reuptake Inhibitors in Pregnant Women and Neonatal Withdrawal Syndrome: A Database Analysis." *The Lancet.* 2005. 3655 (9458): 482–487.

p. 176. National Institute of Mental Health: "The Numbers Count: Mental Illness in America." *Science on Our Minds Fact Sheet Series.* Accessed August 1999.

p. 181. Steiner, M., Steinberg, S., Stewart, D., et al. "Fluoxetine in the Treatment of Premenstrual Dysphoria." *N Engl J Med.* 1995. 332:1529–1534.

p. 189. Lucht, M., Schaub, R., Myer, C., et al. "Gender Differences in Unipolar Depression: A General Population Survey." *Archives of Women's Mental Health.* 2001. 3(suppl 2):62.

Chapter 9

p. 202. Bidlingmaier, F., Strom, T.M., Dorr, G., et al. "Estrone and Estradiol Concentrations in Human Ovaries, Testes, and Adrenals During the First Two Years of Life." *J Clin Endocrinol Metab.* 1987. 65:862–867.

p. 203. DeBellis, M.D., Keshavan, M.S., Beers, S.R., Hall, J., Frutaci, K., Masalehdan, A., Noll, and Boring, A.M. "Sex Differences in Brain Maturation During Childhood and Adolescence." *Cereb Cortex.* 2001. 11(6):552–557.

p. 210. Murphy, D.G.M., DeCarli, C., McIntosh, A.R., et al. "Sex Differences in Human Brain Morphometry and Metabolism: An in vivo Quantitative Magnetic Resonance Impaging and Positron Emission Tomography Study on the Effect of Aging." *Arch Gen Psyhchiatry.* 1996. 53:585–594.

p. 212. Gonzales McNeal, M., Zareparsi, S., Camicioli, R., et al. "Predictors of Healthy Brain Aging." *Journal of Gerontology.* 2001. 56A(7): B294–B301.

Index

Underscored page references indicate boxed text.

m

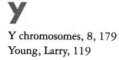

Z